TO LIGHT A CANDLE

TO LIGHT A CANDLE

The Autobiography of James Keller
Founder of The Christophers

1963

Doubleday & Company, Inc.
Garden City, New York

Library of Congress Catalog Card Number 62-15904

CONTENTS

TO LIGHT A CANDLE

CHAPTER I

HOW IT ALL BEGAN

One evening, after giving a talk in Chicago, a man in the audience asked me: "How did you ever happen to start the Christophers?"

His question had a familiar ring, since it had come up hundreds of times and almost invariably in the same words.

The necessarily brief answer that I gave then, and have had to give on most occasions, could only touch on part of the explanation.

Sometimes, in conversations or informal gatherings, the "why and wherefore" of the Christophers could be a little more thoroughly explained, and I could mention some of the many circumstances and people who were instrumental in shaping the idea. Among those I cited most frequently were a young priest in Oakland, California, an old Chinese woman in a leprosarium near Hong Kong, and a group of high school students in Noroton, Connecticut.

One man who was particularly intrigued by what he had heard of these and other influences was John Delaney, an editor of Doubleday & Company.

He kept urging me to write a book on "how it all began." He said countless readers would be interested in knowing what had given the impetus and direction to the person behind the movement.

My first reaction was one of misgiving. I had doubts about

the number of people who would care about such biographical details.

Mr. Delaney, however, was pleasantly insistent. He met my objections by pointing out that the Christopher idea reaches millions of people of all faiths and backgrounds through *Christopher News Notes,* books, telecasts and radio programs—and that many might be further influenced by the positive, hopeful approach of the movement if they knew the "what, when, where, why and how" of its origin and growth.

His reasoning finally convinced me that writing a record of my experiences would be one more opportunity to encourage others to do their part, with God's help, to change the world for the better.

And so these recollections are submitted with the hope that they will fulfill this aim as well as answer the question: "How did you ever happen to start the Christophers?"

New York City has been my home base for more than thirty years, although it is a continent away from Oakland, California, where I was born on June 27, 1900. I have always felt that starting life at the beginning of the twentieth century was both a blessing and a challenge.

In the early years of the century, life was a peaceful affair, at least for me. I spent all of my remembered childhood in one house on Sixteenth Street in Oakland. And when I think back on those years, I can see them as clearly as though tonight I could be climbing the narrow stairway from the kitchen to the large bedroom I shared with my brother Louis.

It was a thoroughly comfortable house. The plot it stood on was a bit on the narrow side, but we had both a front and back yard. An alleyway led down one side of the house to the kitchen door, and our back yard was somewhat formidably surrounded by a high wooden fence.

Back yards in those days invariably had those sturdy,

tightly built, six-foot walls of wood. Frequently a board or two was missing, as if for the greater convenience of youngsters like me who often felt the need for short cuts. Sometimes these knot-holed fences were painted or whitewashed, but more often they were merely gray from the weather.

Our fence served at least two purposes. It protected the two apricot trees from which Mother "put up" the fruit each year. It also provided a vantage point from which to look into the adjacent, similarly walled and sometimes boy-inhabited property on the other side. Climbing up the fence and cautiously making my way along it was always something of an adventure. Now and then, when certain of my activities caused my usually patient mother to put her foot down, I was told in no uncertain terms, "Stay in your own back yard!" And stay there I did. But I always felt that even that order permitted me to survey the surrounding territory from the top of the fence.

This natural inclination to go beyond my own back yard often got me into trouble. I remember one escapade, when I was about eight or nine, that resulted in my "yard arrest" for several days. There was a new apartment building going up a few blocks away, and it was like a magnet to all the neighborhood youngsters. Any construction site, with its stacks of lumber, piles of bricks, cement-mixing tubs and shouting workmen, ranks just short of paradise for small boys. This one had an added attraction—an elevator—which was a rather new thing in those days.

One day when no one was around, I persuaded one of my pals that we ought to give the thing a try. We made our way into the nearly completed building and, after a few experimental bounces, got the elevator going.

We were in the midst of our joy ride when we heard the building manager shouting at us. We thought that if we just kept riding up and down, he couldn't catch us. But he simply pushed the call button for his floor, and when the doors opened, there we were—caught red-handed.

We were hauled off to our respective parents, and I don't know how my partner fared, but I think a few hours passed before I cared to sit down anywhere. I accepted my confinement to the back yard with considerable meekness.

While the back yard always held a certain fascination, the front one was a different story, and mainly because of the steps that led up to our front porch. It was my chore to keep them clean. Boylike, I usually tried to get away with just a lick and a promise, but what made me think I could succeed is hard to figure. Mother always called me back to scrub those steps over again. I have learned since to bless her for this lesson in thoroughness.

The house itself was a comfortable, two-story frame structure, painted gray. It had a front and back parlor, a dining room and kitchen on the first floor, and four bedrooms on the second. It was well suited to meet the needs of my father, mother and us six children.

The parlors were somewhat formal rooms. Each one had a fireplace, equipped with gas logs which were lit only on the special occasions when the rooms were used.

Electricity was not yet in widespread use and, like most of the houses in Oakland, gas was used for lighting as well as for the fireplaces. I can still hear the slight hissing of those open jets.

I can also still clearly picture the dining room, with the big round table and straight-backed chairs, all made of dark oak, and the large mirrored china closet that displayed a set of bright flowered dishes.

The large kitchen was the most actively used room in the Keller household. It was the very center of things, and the spot where most of us were to be found when we were at home. We played games as well as did our homework on the kitchen table and, of course, had family meals and discussions there. In those days, kitchens were equipped simply. The major items were the stoves (we had two—a gas range and a wood-burning one) and a table and chairs. The sink was in the pantry. Today, such an arrangement would probably be called a kitchen-family room.

Feeding a family of our size was a pretty large order, and I had a typical growing-boy's appetite. When Mother gave us pancakes for breakfast, it was all she could do to keep them coming fast enough.

Two flights of stairs led to the second floor—one from the front hall, and a narrower one next to the kitchen. Upstairs, we children shared three of the four bedrooms. My sister Hazel was the oldest—ten years older than I—while Mildred was the "baby." Of the four boys, Harold and Louis were older than I, and Reginald was about two years younger. Because our ages were so close, Louis and I shared more than our bedroom—we played together and joined forces at such household chores as Mother prevailed on us to do.

My brother Harold spent very little time at home. He had contracted tuberculosis when he was seventeen and, from then on, lived mostly at a sanitorium in the mountains, where he died several years later.

Like most children, I didn't think much about my parents' early lives. I unconsciously assumed that the circumstances in which I knew them had always existed. Since my life parted from theirs a bit earlier than most children's, I never did learn much about their childhood.

My father, whom I was named after, was a sturdy, smooth-shaven man of medium height. He was born in Ireland, one of several sons of a family named Kelleher. At the age of eighteen, he came to America. He had been preceded by an uncle who found the name Kelleher a little difficult for his

American business friends to spell and pronounce. So he changed it to Keller. The shorter version apparently appealed to my father, too, for he adopted it and our family has used it ever since.

After reaching America in the 1880s, Father eventually followed his uncle to Oakland. During the land boom of the '80s, the railroads, with large blocks of land to sell, used low fares as an enticement to draw people out from the East and Midwest. This may have been what lured young Irishmen to this new land of milk and honey. There in California, to his great good fortune, my father met and married Margaret Selby.

Mother's family had originated in Chicago and had moved West while she was still a young girl.

The early years of my parents' married life must have been moderately prosperous, for at the time of my earliest recollections, Father owned a successful "men's furnishings" store at Tenth and Broadway in Oakland. Originally it had been a partnership, and the store operated under the name of Keller and Fitzgerald. But Father eventually bought out his partner, and the store, as I knew it, carried his name alone.

It was twelve blocks from home, so until I was eight or nine, I seldom visited it. But then, since my older brother, Louis, was busy with his paper route, I was drafted part-time to wrap packages and keep the sidewalk clean. I got to know it intimately and could soon promptly put my hand on any item of its varied stock.

Though the store carried only men's furnishings, these did not include suits. "Haberdashery" is probably the correct word for it. Shirts, ties, collars, hats, socks, underwear, handkerchiefs and other small articles were all there on display. I especially remember the considerable assortment of stiffly starched collars. There were many different styles and sizes, arranged on the shelves in square yellow boxes. They sold two for a quarter, and customers nearly always bought them in quantities. It was something of a trick to roll half a dozen collars up snugly and keep them meticulously clean while wrapping them. Though the better part of a half century has passed since I was last called upon for such a task, I suspect I could still do it.

The store was open every weekday from eight in the morning till six, except Saturday nights when, along with most others, it stayed open until ten. All his life, my father followed an early-to-bed, early-to-rise routine and was rarely away from his store during business hours.

Father was a naturally quiet sort of man. But being Irish, he had a good sense of humor, which we all enjoyed and hoped would rub off on us. Because his work kept him away from home for the greater part of the day and into the evening, it fell to Mother to become not only the directing head of the house in his absence, but also the moving spirit.

In those days, I never thought about Mother's age. She was in her thirties when I was a little fellow, but to me she was ageless and tireless. She seemed to give no thought at all to herself. She was the first one up and the last to bed, and no matter how unexpected some new development might be, she always seemed able to cope with it. We could always rely on her patient understanding and love. And, of course, we took it all for granted.

I remember once trying to escape a spanking by dashing up the back stairs and racing along the second-floor hallway to go down the front and out the door to safety. But quick-witted Mother had stationed my sister Hazel at the escape route. I was trapped and, of course, got the spanking. Whenever any of us six children ran to her for help or comfort, though, we got that too.

When I was about five years old, a friend of Mother's jokingly asked her if she had adopted me. I suppose I was a bit of a contrast, being slight and dark while all the other children were sturdy and fair. To my childish ears, though, that remark was not the slightest bit amusing. It was a deadly serious piece of news. I can remember to this day how distressed and lost I felt. If I didn't belong here . . . if this wasn't my family . . . how did I get here and where *did* I belong? I began to look at my brothers and sisters with a sort of awe; they were the real thing—I was the intruder. This went on for several days until Mother must have noticed that something was bothering me. She took me in her lap and said something like, "What's the matter with my little Jamie?" After sobbing out my troubled heart, she gave me the reassurance I had been longing for.

Though many happenings of those early years are vivid memories, they usually don't fall into a specific time slot. There were a few exceptions, however. One was an event that took place just two months and nine days before my sixth birthday.

We had all gone to bed on the evening of April 17, 1906, without the slightest thought that anything unusual was about to occur. But a few minutes past five the following morning, I remember being awakened by the bed swaying in a most uncanny way. Sounds that I had never heard before reverberated in frightening profusion. Timbers creaked and creaked again. From the kitchen below came the clatter of falling pots and pans, and from the pantry and dining room the unmistakable sound of breaking dishes. Suddenly from somewhere above our heads came a fearfully heavy crash. It turned out to be our brick chimney—it had collapsed, pitched over the eaves, and crashed heavily to the ground beside the basement wall.

Before I knew it we were all outside in our night clothes. Up and down the street others were in the same predicament. The chimneys of most of the houses had fallen, patches of shingles had been torn off the roofs, and the eaves were a bit dog-eared and tattered where gutters had broken away.

The first destructive shock had lasted under a minute. Lesser ones followed in quick succession. Frightened though everyone was, we had no idea how extensive or destructive the damage was. We thought at first that the quake had hit only Oakland. But little by little, word began to reach us that other areas had suffered, too. Separated from San Francisco by the five-mile width of the Bay, we had no contact with the greater city except by ferry, so word of what had happened there was slow in reaching us. But within an hour or two, rising columns of smoke told us of fires in the area west of the San Francisco ferry terminal. Before the morning was half over, every ferry that reached the Oakland terminal was crowded to capacity. Thousands of refugees were escaping from the furiously burning city.

For three days almost everyone in Oakland watched the gigantic pall of smoke that rose from the burning city across the Bay. Oakland people did what they could to help, but because the telegraph lines from San Francisco were all down, the rest of the country knew almost nothing of the damage. When at last the fires were brought under control, some twenty-eight thousand buildings had been destroyed and four square miles of San Francisco had been completely devastated.

In the autumn following the earthquake and fire I started school. I was sent to Lafayette, the public school just about a block away from home. During the next eight years, it became as familiar as home. The three-story red-brick building on West Street, between Seventeenth and Eighteenth, is still standing. I suppose there have been some renovations and additions in recent years. Then it had eight classrooms and a manual-training department which occupied part of the basement. The halls—in my memory, at any rate—were large, and the ceilings high. The principal's office was close to the main entrance, and a place for which we had a full share of respect.

The large playground provided plenty of space for the varied activities of several hundred boys and girls. There was little "formal" equipment, other than basketball courts, so we brought along baseballs and bats in the spring, and footballs in the autumn.

Each morning, just before nine o'clock, we lined up by classes outside the main entrance near the flagpole, and marched to our various classrooms to the music of a piano, played by one of the teachers.

Since grade-school teachers give us our first glimpse of the world beyond the family, they usually stand out in the memories of all of us. Many of those at Lafayette were only in their early twenties, but they worked hard and demanded our respect. They were really interested in the children in their classes and were strong on spelling, grammar, composition, arithmetic and discipline, to the great advantage of their pupils.

I remember Miss Morris—short, slender and pleasant—an especially zealous worker who took no nonsense when it came to studying. Many was the afternoon spent "after school" for trying to skip over a lesson here or there. Then there was Miss Lisson, who was somewhat prim. Her skirts and blouses were always immaculate and her hair smoothly and securely in place. Her mind was in place, too, and what she taught us we remembered. I still thank Miss McKeever for those hours of drilling in basic arithmetic. Writing out those tables endlessly seemed like a waste of time then, but they gave us a mental discipline that I have since realized could be achieved in no other way.

Miss Hennings stands out in a particular way. Even her glasses shone, and though all our teachers were neat, she took the prize. Her obviously sincere manner and gentle personality are something I have never forgotten.

Young as I was, I had a dim comprehension of the importance of teaching even then, for I couldn't help noticing that it was the teacher who "made" the class. As I grew older, my appreciation of dedicated, competent teachers increased and I came to a far better realization of what an important vocation they have.

School and homework took care of the days and evenings from Monday to Friday. But Saturday and Sunday were different stories.

Part of Saturday was always a work day, and we all had chores to take care of . . . that porch, for instance. One charge that came to each of us in turn was the weekly grocery shopping. Mother was a great one for delegating responsibility to each of us and she fully expected us to measure up to the confidence she placed in us. She was also very "thrift-minded" and tried to show us how to get the best at the most reasonable price.

On the Saturday shopping tours, she used to give us the order and send us to the other side of town to the Washington Market. There, individual merchants had stalls where they sold their fresh fruits and vegetables, and there was a separate section for the meat department. Mother always expected us to do a little comparison shopping and not buy the first cantaloupe, bunch of grapes, or carrots we saw.

I remember one somewhat embarrassing lesson that came from one of my shopping turns. Chops happened to be one of the items on my list for that day, and I came home thinking I had completed my trip to the market very successfully. When the packages were opened, however, Mother discovered I had one less chop than I should have had for the amount I had paid. So back she sent me to tell the butcher that there had been an error and I had not received the full order. I didn't forget that experience in a hurry, and it taught me a lesson in values that has stood me in good stead many a time since.

Though we often grumbled about having to take time out of our "free" day to do such chores, we really were quite delighted to be given "grownup" responsibilities, and I have always been grateful to Mother for that practical training she gave us in doing an efficient and independent job.

After our weekly chores were done, we were on our own. Like most boys, I was always looking for a little supplement to my allowance and found that Grandmother Selby could usually provide a few jobs that "paid." Mine usually turned out to be watering the lawn. She lived in a corner house, just three blocks from ours. She also owned four neighboring houses which she rented to tenants, so between the five places there was plenty of grass to keep green. Although I was anxious for the payment, I was just as anxious to get the work over with and often tried to do a quick and not too thorough job. But Grandmother almost invariably glanced out the window at the wrong moment and reminded me that I had neglected a few spots.

Like all grandmothers, she always generously produced a little "extra bonus" when the job was done, but she was quite aware of the value of being strict and making us realize that we had better not take on anything we weren't going to make every effort to do well.

Sunday was family day, starting out with eight o'clock Mass in our "best." Afterwards, the children stayed behind for Sunday school. Those of us who were old enough then went on to Grandmother Selby's to join the grownups for a family breakfast-lunch.

After being on our best behavior for a few hours, we were always delighted when the time came for Father's walk.

Those long treks he took with the boys were always a high point of the day, especially since we never had to go too far before he stopped to buy us some candy.

Every summer for some years, our whole family left Oakland behind and went to our small summer cottage at Inverness on Tomales Bay, about thirty miles north of the Golden Gate. Father joined us for weekends, but the rest of us moved en masse for the summer. We first took the ferry across San Francisco Bay, then another to Sausalito and, finally, a train the rest of the way.

The countryside around Inverness was attractive and comparatively undeveloped in those days. Our cottage was set up for casual summer living. It had a rambling porch with hammocks and comfortable wicker furniture. The interior consisted of a small kitchen, two bedrooms and a large and simply furnished living room which doubled as a dining room.

Since we were only about a mile from the water, we all learned to swim when we were about six or seven. I remember having one close shave during the learning process. I wasn't far from shore, but I stepped into a hole that put me over my head. It seemed like an eternity while I coughed and spluttered and tried to flail myself out of the predicament. But it probably was only a matter of seconds before a lady who was in the water nearby saw what was happening. She grabbed me by the hair and hauled me out.

I was afraid that I wouldn't be allowed back in the water if I told anyone about my experience. So it wasn't until months later that Mother heard about it. By then I was better able to keep afloat.

We fished a good deal, too. We didn't have a boat of our own but could always find friends to take us out.

The arrival of sharks in the Bay always caused great excitement. They were never large, but when we spotted their triangular dorsal fins approaching the pier, which wasn't far from our house, we hurried to bait our big shark hook. This sturdy bit of equipment was made fast to a line that was much heavier than what we used for normal fishing. We fastened a big piece of meat to the end of it and dangled it in the water. When we got a bite, the fun began. We had to hang onto the line as the fish whipped back and forth. The biggest shark we landed was only about five feet, but it still was well equipped with teeth. More often than not, the sharks succeeded in getting away.

My brother Louis and I had a few daily chores—one of which was to get up early each morning and gather wood for the kitchen stove. Since there were always quantities of fallen branches in the woods behind the house, we didn't have far to go.

Aside from a few other tasks, just as simple, we had little to do all summer but enjoy ourselves.

When we were at Inverness, we went to Mass every Sunday at a little local chapel. During the rest of the year, as I mentioned, the family attended Mass each Sunday morning at St. Francis de Sales Church at Nineteenth and Grove streets in Oakland, a dozen blocks or so from home. It was—and still is —a handsome red-brick building, solidly built, Gothic in design, and capable of accommodating about a thousand people. When Auxiliary Bishop Floyd L. Begin of Cleveland was appointed Bishop of Oakland in February, 1962, he named St. Francis de Sales as his cathedral. This is the church where the big events of our lives took place. We children received our first Holy Communion and Confirmation there, and long after I had left home, it was the scene of a special event of my own.

I remember my Confirmation for a particular reason. This sacrament, administered by a bishop, includes the Sign of the Cross traced on the forehead, and a light tap on the cheek, reminding the Christian that he should be willing to suffer for his faith. All the boys of the Confirmation class went to the altar to receive the Sacrament from Auxiliary Bishop Edward J. Hanna. When my turn came I heard the bishop say the Latin words of Confirmation over my head, felt the oil of chrism placed on my forehead in the Sign of the Cross, and then I immediately got up to leave before being tapped on the cheek. With a twinkle in his eye, the bishop called me back to "get my suffering," as he put it. Bishop Hanna, who later became Archbishop of San Francisco, had a significant effect on my life on two more occasions years later.

The catechism classes we went to right after Mass when we were growing up were conducted largely by the lay people of the parish. Quite often, though, one of the young curates stopped in to aid in our instruction.

I remember one of these visits with great clarity. There were six rows of seats in the room and I was sitting on the window side in the fourth seat of the row farthest to the young curate's right. Though I was only six at the time, one statement that he made still stands vividly among my recollections.

"One of you little fellows," he said, "may be a priest some day and do some good for the world." I certainly didn't understand all the implications of his remark, but I distinctly remember ducking beneath my desk, hoping that the young priest who stood before us didn't mean me!

At one time or another, most of us come to turning points without being aware of it. As I look back on it now, I'm convinced that the young curate's remark gave my life's work its first impetus.

Little did I dream that years later I would be echoing that same divine challenge, trying to remind countless persons that each of us, regardless of who or where he is, has a mission in life "to do some good for the world."

CHAPTER II

IN AND OUT OF THE SEMINARY

For the next six or seven years, my life followed a normal course. Each autumn I returned to Lafayette School and, though my marks were not much above the average, I was always promoted.

Along with other boys in school, I learned to ride a bicycle and was eventually given one of my own.

Shortly after that, a friend and I mapped out a round-trip bike ride of "only" 160 miles. The first leg was south down to San Jose, about 50 miles, then over to Santa Cruz on the coast. From San Jose to Santa Cruz is only 29 miles, but it involves crossing over some hilly country. Once we reached Santa Cruz, we planned to go up the coast route for 81 miles to San Francisco. From there the last lap would be the nickel ferry ride across the Bay back to Oakland.

It seemed like a very reasonable trip to us, but not to any-one else. "Where will you sleep? . . . What will you eat? . . . How do you expect to get across those hills?" we were asked. Our spirits were not in the least dampened by the prediction that we'd be heading for home by nightfall.

With about a dollar and a half between us, my friend and I set out early one morning. We had packed sandwiches, but they were gone in the first few hours. After that, we had to depend on our wits and the generosity of farmers, who gave us peaches and apricots from their groves and water from their wells.

We reached San Jose in the early evening, but decided not to stop there. We wanted to tackle that mountain stretch in the morning and figured the closer we could get to it that night, the fresher we'd be for the hardest part of our trip. We pedaled on for about ten miles, but soon it was too dark to see. We began looking around for a place to sleep and finally found a small building with a covered porch. There were no lights, but on close inspection it turned out to be a one-room schoolhouse. We stretched out on the hard floor of the porch for the night. If not exactly comfortable, we were at least sheltered. When we awoke very early the next morning and got our bearings, we found we were just outside Los Gatos, with the foothills straight in front of us. We headed up them right away.

It was painful, slogging footwork—but we enjoyed every wearisome minute. We dragged our bicycles up miles and miles of winding, curving roads. Going downhill was a little easier. At least we could ride, but since neither of us had coaster brakes, we had to drag one foot on the ground or keep one foot on the front wheel to check our speed.

We arrived in Santa Cruz about 8:30 in the morning. It had taken some three hours to cover the up-and-down route. Needless to say, we were ready for breakfast. And, at this point, our meager funds had dwindled considerably.

We found a pleasant little cafe in Santa Cruz with a sign proclaiming "Breakfast Rolls—5¢ Each." We decided we could afford two each. So we went in and seated ourselves at one of the little tables that was set up with cutlery, glasses, paper napkins and a large pitcher of milk. After ordering our rolls we pounced on that pitcher of milk. Taking turns, we had just about drained it when the manager walked over.

"Boys," he said, looking very stern, "that pitcher of milk goes with a twenty-five-cent minimum breakfast order."

It had already "gone"—in the literal sense of the word—with our ten-cent orders! Seeing that our pockets were about as empty as the pitcher, the manager was kind enough not to press the matter. Never before or since has milk tasted so good as it did that morning.

Late that afternoon—less than two days after starting out—we arrived home: tired, dirty and hungry, but triumphant. After a weary hello to Mother, I went straight to bed.

My bicycle continued to play a big part in my life. At ten or eleven years of age, I managed to get a newspaper route, which meant getting up to the clatter of an alarm clock at the unearthly hour of four-thirty and cycling a mile or more downtown to get my papers. With half of them in a cloth "carrying bag" slung over my shoulder and the rest on the handlebars, I headed back, delivering the papers on the way. My arrival home was just about the time Mother had breakfast ready. Even without that early morning ride, my appetite would have been good, but after two hours of hard work, it was enormous.

With four sons, Father quite naturally expected one of us to come into his reasonably prosperous business. Since Harold was trying to recover his health in the mountains, and Reg was a little young at the time, it really boiled down to Louis or me. And for some reason I never understood, since Louis was fully as competent as I, Father concluded that I was the one to join him. But it wasn't until I was thirteen and I began to make plans of my own that his idea came to light.

During these years the thought that the young curate had planted in my unwilling head often returned to me. There were plenty of times when I forgot about it, but the notion was never completely gone. Dreaming as all boys do about the future, I often thought of myself as a priest.

I didn't discuss this with anyone, and actually, the whole idea was still somewhat vague and unreal. Nevertheless something was urging me in the direction I ultimately followed. My steady attendance at daily Mass eventually led to my becoming an altar boy. But since there were quite a few of us at St. Francis de Sales Church, my turn came only about every third or fourth week.

In 1912, when I was in the seventh grade at Lafayette and still serving as an altar boy, a new and very personable young priest by the name of Father Michael Murray came to our church as a curate. He was about twenty-nine—only recently arrived from Ireland—and an immediate "success."

Though it's over fifty years ago, I remember that he seemed unusually tall and slender in his black cassock. His clerical collar was high and he usually wore a square biretta with three projections that radiated from the short tassel in the center. Even when he was most active, his pince-nez firmly retained its grip on the rather high bridge of his nose. He had the air of an aristocrat about him. His hair was very dark, his eyes were brown and, despite his youth, his face was lined in a way that made his maturity obvious without giving him the appearance of age.

He took a real interest in the boys who served Mass, and soon he knew a good deal about us. For, inherently dignified though he was, his manner was so friendly and sympathetic that we were completely at ease with him.

Though five years or more had passed since the earlier curate had said that one of us might some day be a priest, the idea was still very much in the background of my thoughts. In fact, young as I was, it seemed to me only good sense to work hard here for God and others, so my eternity might be spent with the Lord.

Father Murray must have sensed that my thoughts were leaning in this direction, for one day he asked me if I would like to be a priest.

No one had ever actually put the question to me before. But now that it had come, I found myself saying "yes"— though a little hesitantly, I must admit.

I really meant what I said, but at the same time, the hesitancy was real. Perhaps it had to do with a vague feeling of unworthiness and the great responsibilities that would be involved if I chose this course.

Father Murray told me then and in later conversations what I would need to do in order to prepare for the priesthood. He suggested that, when I graduated from eighth grade, if I was still of the same mind, I could apply for entrance to St. Patrick's, the preparatory seminary of the Archdiocese of San Francisco. This was in Menlo Park—twenty-five miles south of San Francisco and a short distance from Stanford University at Palo Alto. It would be necessary, he explained, for me to get permission from my parents. Then if I were accepted, there would be a moderate tuition and certain other costs. He assured me that if I wanted to enter and if my parents agreed, I would most likely be accepted.

Having gone this far, he did not press the matter. We discussed it again from time to time, but he never urged me to make a decision. And I still refrained from discussing the idea with anyone else. But finally, with less than a year before I was to graduate from elementary school and enter the preparatory seminary if I were going to do so, I definitely made up my mind. It was only then—and perhaps I was a bit abrupt about it—that I brought up the subject at home.

It seemed strange that the idea which had been on my mind for so long should have surprised my parents so much. But it did. They knew I attended Mass daily, of course, and that I had been serving as an altar boy for several years. But apparently they had no inkling of my plans for becoming a priest. The idea came to them not only as a surprise but also as one that they were not prepared to accept.

In fact, both Father amd Mother seemed reluctant to give me any encouragement whatever. They did not discuss it very much with me. But it was obvious from their few remarks that they felt I was much too young to be setting my heart on such a big objective. I was only thirteen at the time and, while I probably seemed terribly grownup to myself, I'm sure I was very much a child in their eyes.

Their apparent lack of sympathy may have been their way of testing my sincerity, of trying to make sure that my desire to be a priest was a real vocation and not a passing fancy.

Since neither Father nor Mother took an outright stand against my being a priest, I continued to remind them from time to time that my heart was set on it.

The reaction of the rest of the family—my brothers and sisters, aunts and uncles, and my Grandmother Selby—was surprise more than anything else.

"Jim? Jim wants to be a priest? A priest?"

They seemed to feel that for someone who could have had a secure and steady future in a successful family business, I was showing a considerable lack of balance.

But, despite the bewilderment, there seemed to be a little touch of pride at the idea of having a priest in the family.

Father sent Mother over to St. Francis de Sales Church to have a talk with Father Murray. I don't know what was said in that conversation, but I imagine the air was well cleared on both sides. Anyway, a few months later when I told Mother and Father that I still wanted to go to St. Patrick's, they gave their reluctant consent and agreed to pay the tuition and other incidental costs.

Father Murray wrote a recommendation to the seminary, and during the summer I received a letter from St. Patrick's saying that my application had been accepted.

In the early autumn of 1914, with my various belongings in a trunk and suitcase (presented to me by Grandmother Selby), I took the ferry to San Francisco, where I caught a local Southern Pacific train for Menlo Park, and finally a taxi from the station to the seminary.

My first impressions as I rode up the curving gravel drive to the school were of the physical beauty of the grounds and the handsome three-story red-brick building. It was designed in the shape of the letter "E." The central arm contained the main chapel, and the other two had classrooms, study rooms, and student living quarters. One end was for the minor seminary which, as a beginner, I was about to enter. The other was for the major seminary, where students who had completed the preparatory course lived. The front of the building, which formed the "backbone" of the "E," contained offices and reception rooms, as well as quarters for the faculty.

The grounds covered the better part of a hundred level acres. There were many well-kept flower beds, large numbers of handsome palm and other trees, and off in the distance a baseball diamond, as well as tennis, basketball and handball courts. As I climbed the broad flight of granite steps to the main entrance of the seminary, I tried to remember how I should act and what Father Murray had told me to do.

I made my way inside and asked where I could find Father John J. Doran, the rector of the minor seminary. Then, hat in hand, I entered his office and in a small voice introduced myself.

Father Doran could be solemn on occasion, I later learned, but he was genial and kind in welcoming me, and called one of the students to help me get settled in my quarters. In spite of the rector's warm reception, I felt a little lost. But my pride, along with having another boy show me around, helped me fight down that sinking feeling. Afterwards, events came so swiftly I didn't have time for homesickness.

There were dormitories on the second and third floors. "New" boys were all assigned to the third-floor quarters, which measured about fifty feet in width and a good deal more than that in length. Quite a change from the bedroom I had shared with my brother at home!

The dormitory was simply furnished and without ornament, except for a large crucifix on one wall. Each boy, in addition to his cot, had only a plain straight chair and a wooden locker to hold his possessions. One corner of the dormitory had been partitioned off to form a small separate room which was occupied by the prefect. With about sixty-five of us, the need for a supervisor to control our youthful energy was obvious.

I have sometimes wondered if any other creature in all the world is half so adaptable as the average boy. I clearly remember how ill at ease I was on my day of arrival and how homesick I felt that first night. Yet, before the first week was over I found myself part and parcel of the place and quite at home.

Of all the new experiences that were soon to become daily routine, I think our mealtimes were the hardest to get used to. At home it always had been the time for family conversation, and we all eagerly awaited our chance to tell the others what had happened during the day. But here, several hundred of us sat together in the big dining room, with no one speaking a word. While we ate, one of the seminarians chosen for the day read aloud from an elevated rostrum, first from the Scriptures and then from the life of a saint. The major seminarians sat silently on one side of the large room, while we students of the minor seminary sat quietly on the other side. The dozen or more Sulpician Fathers who were our faculty ate at a long table of their own—also without a word. For the first few days, we new boys were subject to fits of

smothered giggles, as youngsters generally are when under restraint and in new situations.

But gradually we began to realize that this rule not only
encouraged a certain amount of self-discipline and control but
also taught us the spirit of silence—the enriching values of
quiet reflection and contemplation, uncomplicated by speech.

Breakfast was the only meal at which we were allowed to
talk. The exception was probably made because we had already
been up for nearly two hours by then and the Fathers thought
we wouldn't survive without an outlet. We used to rise to
the ringing of bells at 5:30. Morning prayers and meditation
were in a large prayer hall, and we attended Mass in the
chapel at 6:20, followed by a study period from 6:45 to 7:15,
and only then that marvelous pleasure—breakfast. Afterwards,
there was a short recreation period, and then classes began.

Because the course of study in the preparatory seminary
covered six years, it was the equivalent of the ordinary high
school plus junior college. We had classes in English, various
branches of science, history, and church history, Latin, Greek,
French, mathematics and public speaking. There were study
periods every day and a recreation period each afternoon,
during which we could walk or play baseball, tennis, basketball or handball.

Just before supper there was a period set aside for spiritual
reading. Afterwards, the evening was divided into recreation,
study, and night prayers in the chapel. Late hours were unknown at St. Patrick's. By 9:30 we were in bed with lights out.

We had a two-week Christmas holiday and a three-month
summer vacation. Throughout the school year, however, the
seminary program left little time unscheduled. Since the seminary serves as preparation for the priesthood, a religious atmosphere naturally pervaded the entire place. Yet, except for
the important difference that we seminarians were already
aiming towards our life work, we were much the same as

schoolboys everywhere. We swarmed over the baseball diamond and the tennis and handball courts during our recreation periods. I was as eager as the next in playing games. But I eventually got most of my exercise chopping wood—an activity I thoroughly enjoyed and enthusiastically recommend for all-around physical development.

The student body at St. Patrick's Seminary ranged in age from about fourteen to twenty-six, but the older and younger boys had comparatively few contacts with each other. The older students, who seemed very grownup to the rest of us, lived a separate existence in the major seminary. Their advanced courses covered another six years of study, and the schedule they followed was necessarily different. Except at mealtime, we didn't see much of them. Two other things set them apart and made us long for the day when we would join their ranks: they wore cassocks, as did the priests, and each had a room of his own.

My first three years at St. Patrick's went by without incident and I was confident that I had made the right decision in studying for the priesthood.

The fourth year began in the autumn of 1917. Though life at the seminary continued in the same pattern, we could not help but be touched by the unsettled times. The United States had just entered World War I, and my brother Louis, cousins and friends were volunteering or being drafted for service overseas.

This stress probably played a big part in the second thoughts I began to have. Looking back, I can't even be sure what those doubts were or when I first became conscious of them. There weren't any specific reasons I could put my finger on. But nevertheless, there they were. I didn't realize it at the time, but this confusion within my own heart and mind was more or less the same turmoil that nearly every young person goes

through in one form or another when he is about to embark
on his life's work.

These doubts stuck with me through the fall term and by
Christmas I was pretty well convinced that I had better look
for a new course. Then something else happened that further
influenced my decision.

My mother's two brothers, Albert and Walter Selby, ran a
very profitable chewing-gum factory, as well as a candy store
and soda fountain called Selby's, in San Francisco. It was
located on Market Street across from the Emporium and
not far from where the Powell Street cable car has its Market
Street terminus.

Their store was quite a large one. It was long and narrow,
with a soda fountain on one side and an attractive, well-
stocked candy counter on the other. Tables were in the rear.
It was a very busy place and had some thirty employees on
its payroll.

Of the two businesses, the chewing-gum factory was by far
the more important, and both my uncles devoted most of
their time to it. In fact, my father had decided to close up his
own business and join my uncles as manager of their thriving
factory.

The candy store, which was open from nine in the morning
until eleven at night, was under the direction of a woman
manager whose hands were more than full. My uncles had
finally reached the conclusion that she needed an associate
manager.

When I got home for Christmas, I began to hear all about
this. No one thought to suggest me as a possibility, since I
was only seventeen and a half, and my future seemed settled
anyway.

But in the absence of any other idea, the prospect of helping manage a big candy store in San Francisco seemed challenging. When my uncles learned of my interest, they offered

me the job and I took it. My doubts, by this time, had so increased that even without this offer, I did not intend to go back to St. Patrick's. I sent a letter to the rector, notifying him with regret that I would not return to the seminary after Christmas vacation.

And so began my career as a San Francisco "businessman."

CHAPTER III

IN AND OUT OF THE CANDY STORE

The usual pre-Christmas rush was on, so I went right to work. Each morning I took an interurban train to the Oakland ferry terminal. After the pleasant five-mile ride across the Bay, I took a streetcar up Market Street for the last leg of the daily trip to the candy store.

While I was in the seminary, Father had bought a house on Lenox Avenue near Lake Merritt, only a block from where the interurban trains ran along Lake Shore Boulevard on their way to and from the ferry terminal.

Our new home was a two-story stucco house with a good-sized front and back yard as well as a garage. When he purchased the new house, Father bought the family's first car, too. It was a black Chandler touring car with leather upholstery and a folding top that turned out to be more trouble than it was worth to raise or lower.

The house was much more attractive both inside and out than the old one. On the first floor there was a living room, hall, a dining room, kitchen, and a large sun parlor where the family congregated. Because the house stood on a slope, most of the rooms got lots of sunlight. Upstairs, there were five bedrooms, in addition to a sleeping porch. For the first time in my life, I could boast of a room of my own.

We were all pleased with the house, but my new job on Market Street kept me away from it most of the time. I was

at the store six days a week, and with commuting back and
forth, I didn't have much spare time. But since I had been
accustomed to a somewhat demanding schedule, I was not
especially bothered by my new one. And, no matter how often
I took the trip across the Bay, I always enjoyed the long ferry
ride.

Because the candy store was open from nine in the morning
to eleven at night, my associate manager and I alternated our
shifts. When I first went to work, however, it was my job to
open the store each morning. This, I discovered, amounted to
a lot more than merely unlocking the door. I had to get there
well before we were ready for business, in order to open the
safe and cash register, see that supplies were taken out and
prepared for use and that the candy counter was properly
set up. Everything had to be neat, attractive and scrupulously
clean.

Those were the days before the widespread use of automatic
refrigeration, and one of the employees had to spend a lot of
time each morning chopping and distributing large amounts
of ice. I don't remember exactly how much we used, but I'll
never forget the big 300-pound blocks that the ice wagon delivered daily. They were skidded across the sidewalk by the
husky icemen and then, by way of a steel trap door that
opened in the sidewalk near the building line, the heavy cakes
disappeared into the basement. There they were chopped into
small pieces and put in tubs for use at the soda fountain and
in the power-driven ice cream freezers.

The candy we sold was made on the premises, but there
were far too many kinds to provide new supplies of each one
daily. As a result, the candy makers, of whom we usually
employed three, made only a few varieties on any given day.
Except for specialties, they made enough to last for several
days.

Selby's was an attractive place, especially to anyone with a sweet tooth. Its products were high in quality and the employees who "waited on the trade" were courteous, well trained and neatly uniformed. Usually there were two or three white-jacketed young men at the soda fountain, and two similarly clad bus boys who kept the tables and soda fountain clean and orderly. There was usually enough business to keep five or six waitresses on the go. Each one wore a small, crisp white apron over a neat black dress. Except for rush periods, two uniformed girls could handle the candy counter.

The cashier, and the two of us who were now serving as co-managers, rounded out the staff which directly served the store's patrons. The public rarely saw those who worked behind the scenes. Yet however busy the store itself might be, the basement was busier still.

It was larger than the store space. An additional area that lay below a neighboring store had been rented and a very efficient layout had been developed. There was a well-equipped candy kitchen and, next to it, a room where long tables were set up for several adept chocolate dippers and packers. The dippers sat in front of huge kettles of chocolate that were warmed over gas plates.

Their fingers were constantly in and out of the rich, warm, chocolate. As each different kind of candy was dipped, it was set aside to harden, and was decorated by a twist of the wrist in a special pattern that marked its "kind."

Almost equally skilled were the girls who speedily inserted the thousands of pieces of candy into fragile paper cups before the finished product ended up in gaily decorated boxes on the counter upstairs.

The ice cream freezers were in the basement, too, but usually one man could operate them. Altogether, about ten or twelve persons worked in the production department from nine to six. After six, only a small kitchen was kept opened to prepare sandwiches and other simple dishes for the night trade.

In those days, even the best Selby candy sold for only fifty or sixty cents a pound. Very special boxes such as those for Valentine's Day were sometimes priced a little higher. Candy was usually sold loose rather than in boxes, and small sales predominated—in the ten- to twenty-five-cent category. Fifteen-cent sodas and sundaes were the backbone of the fountain business, though a few customers ordered more extravagant ones. Bulk sales of ice cream were not very frequent then since many people made their own at home and, without dry ice or insulated packages, store containers couldn't travel far. When an occasional person did ask for a pint or even a quart, one of the men at the soda fountain would pack it in a thin cardboard container. Full measure was the rule, and the pasteboard top always bulged noticeably.

Though Selby's was quite different from Father's establishment in Oakland, I soon found that the experience and training he had given me as general factotum in men's furnishings was very helpful. Working for him had not prepared me, however, for handling a large payroll. As a boy still under eighteen, I had much to learn about hiring, firing, promoting and paying those who worked at Selby's. But even that was not as much of a headache as some of the everyday details that had to be mastered—and quickly!

My uncles frequently impressed on me that literally everything had to be checked and rechecked to the very last detail. Here again, as in Father's store, the importance of thoroughness in carrying out seemingly insignificant details was drummed into me. These lessons were to stand me in good stead in pursuing apostolic goals later on.

For instance, we had to be fairly exact in ordering coffee rolls. These weren't made on the premises, and it was essential to estimate our needs precisely so that only the smallest number would be left over to grow stale and unprofitable in our bread box.

Milk and eggs, which also had to be fresh, were just as carefully watched. Though such basic supplies as sugar, nuts and flavoring extracts don't spoil quickly, our supplies of these had to be checked frequently, too.

Besides the candy stockroom, there was another for wrapping paper, boxes and other such supplies. It was important that there be enough on hand for current needs, without tying up capital unnecessarily. Though my uncles were seldom about the place, they never forgot that "the profit is in little things" and demanded that their employees act accordingly.

Once Christmas was over, Selby's grew a bit less hectic and, soon after, I had the routine mastered pretty well.

Though my parents had not been too pleased at first with my plan to study for the priesthood, they had grown accustomed to the idea in the three and a half years I was at St. Patrick's. They were disappointed when I left the seminary. But, as before, they accepted the decision I had made.

Father Murray was equally surprised at my switch but, like my parents, he never pressed me to reconsider. I tried to see him once a week, and I continued to go to daily Mass as often as I could.

My eighteenth birthday was still a few months off but I felt—as most boys my age did in 1918—that I should be in uniform. The German submarine threat which had so endangered the Allies in 1917 was largely under control, but Germany did not seem ready to quit. She launched a powerful new offensive in March 1918, this time on land, and the newspapers were filled with discouraging stories of its advance. One day I went to a recruiting office and applied, but nothing ever came of it. I never learned why I wasn't accepted, but perhaps it was my age, or the fact that the end of the war was in sight.

By early spring, the challenge of working at Selby's seemed to pale a bit. What had been rather exciting in the beginning became routine and monotonous. I began to wonder whether I had made a wise decision after all in leaving the seminary and entering a field so very different from the one for which I had originally prepared.

Turning various supplies into attractive and salable products, and keeping the operations of the business smooth and profitable still held a certain challenge. But it became more and more evident that this type of work didn't offer the satisfaction that I was looking for in my life's work. Somehow, this just didn't seem to be my niche.

Right there on Market Street, it was easy to see a cross-section of successful businesses—yet none of them held any great appeal for me.

At first such thoughts were rare and something less than clear. But though vague and infrequent, they showed no signs of going away.

For years—even though they had been boyhood ones—I had definitely looked forward to becoming a priest. I could still plainly see that priestly work offered a unique opportunity, as the curate had said when I was six or seven, "to do some good for the world." And gradually I began to realize that, when all was said and done, my vocation in life was to be a priest.

One evening, during the period of struggle with myself, a priest came into the store and ordered a sundae. I didn't know him personally, but I had seen him and knew his name. He was Father Ryan, and had been ordained only a few years. Probably because I felt more troubled than ever, I approached him and introduced myself.

There weren't many customers in the store and apparently

he was in no hurry, so we talked for some time. I told him that I had attended St. Patrick's Preparatory Seminary for three and a half years but had decided to leave a few months earlier. When he had finished his sundae, I followed him right out to the sidewalk to continue our conversation. The scene comes back to me vividly.

It was about nine o'clock and Market Street, broad and brightly lighted, had very little traffic on it. About fifty yards away, a Powell Street cable car was being pushed around on its little turntable, with four or five potential passengers lending a hand. Across the way, the show windows of the Emporium were bright, and on our side of the street the passers-by paid little attention to the hatless fellow in earnest conversation with the priest.

Left to himself, Father Ryan would probably have long since been on his way. But I kept the conversation going because the thought was nagging at me that perhaps I should make another try at the priesthood. Since I was halfway resisting the thought, I may have been hoping that Father Ryan would tell me to "stay put."

"I've about decided," I told him, "not to go back."

And then, in the hope that he would back me up, I asked him if he didn't agree that my decision was wise.

To my surprise, he emphatically replied: "No, I'm not going to take it on my conscience to tell you not to go back to the seminary! After all, in God's plan, there may be thousands of people whose salvation depends on what you may do for them as a priest."

He may have said more, but that statement was enough. I don't remember our parting, and I never had another chance to talk intimately with him before he died two or three years later. But the point both he and Father Murray emphasized left a deep and deciding impression on me. In the words of Our Lord, it was: "You have not chosen Me, but I have

chosen you." (John 15:16.) I began to see that failure on my
part to be an instrument of the divine plan could, in a minor
way at least, deprive others of blessings that rightfully belonged to them and that were to be sent through one person
like myself.

This profound thought has continued to affect me ever
since. I have repeatedly referred to it in Christopher talks,
writings and broadcasts, stressing that "there is no substitute
for you in fulfilling the mission in life that Almighty God has
assigned to you and you alone."

Yet, throughout the spring of 1918 this problem continued
to plague me. I saw Father Murray frequently and, though
he still made no attempt to urge me one way or the other, I
felt sure he was anxious to see me return to St. Patrick's. At
last, late in May I made my decision. Father Ryan's incisive
remark had tipped the scales.

But making up my mind didn't solve everything. I had left
St. Patrick's at Christmas and by now had missed one whole
semester. Even if I were permitted to return, where would I
stand in relation to my class?

I told Father Murray what I wanted to do and he suggested
that I study during the summer. I spent every minute I could
spare on the books. By September, my application to return
was accepted, and I passed the special examination which
made me a fully accredited member of my class.

I was delighted to get back to Menlo Park, even though
I know now that the eight months I spent at Selby's with
the candies and sodas was a valuable and useful experience.
(Selby's, incidentally, proved a good training ground for more
than one member of the family. Several years after I had been
there, my brother Louis served a "tour" as assistant manager
before he went into the contracting business.)

I was fortunate to have been reinstated so quickly at St. Patrick's, and doubly so to have been able to rejoin my class. Now still another stroke of good fortune was coming my way —one that affected my whole class.

Two months after we returned to the seminary in the fall of 1918, World War I was over. Suddenly the world found itself unprepared for many peacetime problems. Four long and terribly destructive years had brought drastic changes in the political, economic, social and spiritual lives of entire nations.

The Catholic Church, too, was confronted by many new challenges brought on by the war. One of the most pressing difficulties stemmed from the fact that the fighting had siphoned off many young men who might otherwise have decided to study for the priesthood. And now there was urgent need for more priests than ever. But additional clergy are not as easy to get as additional employees in a business establishment. Even if enrollment in the seminaries increased sharply and immediately, it would still be a dozen years before the new recruits would complete their training.

Something had to be done. The decision for San Francisco lay primarily in the hands of Archbishop Edward J. Hanna. We seminarians, of course, knew little of the discussions being held by the archbishop and seminary officials. But not long after school opened in September, 1918, we were electrified by an unusual announcement.

Some of the classes, mine included, were to be advanced one year to increase the number of priests ordained in the crucial years ahead!

At the time the autumn term began, our class had completed the four years that correspond to high school and had just begun the first year of college work. This new order suddenly made us the equivalent of college sophomores. The number of men entering the major seminary the following year would be just about doubled.

The class we joined wasn't too enthusiastic about our arrival, but we were delighted with the move ahead. I personally gained the most. Not only had I regained my place in class after a one-term absence, but now I was to be advanced an additional year! Life at St. Patrick's appeared brighter than ever.

At first we thought we were simply bypassing a whole year of study. But our stepped-up schedule proved otherwise.

We had hardly settled down to our new scheme of study when, early on the morning of November 11, all the church bells, whistles and sirens within earshot told us that an armistice had been signed in France and that the war was over. We celebrated along with everyone else.

Just about this time, a little party of missionary priests visited St. Patrick's on their way to China. They were part of a new organization, called Maryknoll, or The Catholic Foreign Mission Society of America, with headquarters near Ossining, New York. They had started their work of training priests for missionary work in non-Christian lands in 1911, seven years before. Though they were not widely known then, most students at St. Patrick's knew something of their activities through *The Field Afar*, a periodical which Maryknoll published and sent to our library.

Since these first Maryknollers had only a few days before sailing for the Orient, and many places to cover beforehand, we did not expect to hear or meet them. So when Father Doran came into the study hall to introduce the four China-bound missioners, we were delighted.

The rector paid warm tribute to the vision and faith of this little band, and to the enormous potential of the missionary idea that Maryknoll was fostering throughout the United States.

After introducing Father James E. Walsh, Father Francis

X. Ford and Father Bernard Meyer, he asked the superior of the group and co-founder of Maryknoll, Father Thomas F. Price,* to say a few words. His sincerity and enthusiasm for the pioneer work ahead immediately caught the attention of the 150 students in the study hall.

Father Price said that now it was America's turn to play an active role in the universal mission of the Church and thus tangibly show its gratitude for all that the missioners of Europe had generously given to our own country.

Up to this time, I had given little thought to the idea of working in a foreign land. I knew the Church had much work to do in the United States, but now I began to realize that in our own country almost everyone is at least exposed in some degree to Christianity. It had never before occurred to me so forcibly that, in many parts of the world, countless millions of people have never been given even the slightest opportunity to learn what the teachings of Jesus Christ really are.

As I sat in one corner of the study hall, I was deeply impressed by the forthright manner of these frontier-breaking men of God. The missionary side of the Church suddenly took on a new and deeper meaning. Here were four priests, not merely talking about what should be done, but actually crossing an ocean and continent to fulfill their Christlike conviction and ambition.

*Father Price died in Hong Kong, September 12, 1919, less than a year after leaving the States, following surgery for appendicitis. Father James E. Walsh became the first bishop of Maryknoll in 1927 and the second superior general in 1936. He returned to China in 1948. He was arrested by the Chinese Communists in 1958 and now, in 1963, at the age of 73, is still held prisoner in Shanghai. Father Ford also became a Maryknoll bishop. He died February 21, 1952, in Canton at a hospital attached to the People's National Prison. It is presumed that he died as a result of maltreatment at the hands of his Communist captors. Father Meyer remained in Hong Kong for several years to do relief work, after being freed from a World War II prison camp, and then returned to the United States, where he is writing and distributing catechetical works for mission lands.

CHAPTER IV

ON TO MARYKNOLL

That first year back in the seminary was a busy one. Our accelerated schedule gave us lots to do and little time to do it in.

The next year—1919—at the age of nineteen, I finally entered the major seminary, with six years of specialized training—two of philosophy and four of theology—ahead of me before ordination.

A change of garb and a little more privacy marked the shift from the minor to the major seminary. Along with the black cassock that all the students wore came a small room to call our own. After all those years of living in the goldfish-bowl dormitory, even this tiny cubicle was something special.

The cassock was an ankle-length, closely fitting garment of black medium-weight wool. Except for the shiny black buttons that ran down the front from top to bottom, it was severely plain. With it, we wore a pair of black trousers and a white shirt with a clerical collar.

At Mass, Vespers and Benediction, a white linen surplice with a square-cut neck and elbow-length sleeves was worn over the cassock. Topping all this we wore a black biretta, with three raised ridges radiating from the center of the crown and a short, round tassel.

Although everybody else in the major seminary was wearing the same cassock, I remember feeling pretty self-conscious the first time I put it on.

But as Father Henry Ayrinhac, the rector, celebrated Mass in the chapel and later led us in prayers, I felt a sense of belonging—I felt that I had "arrived," cassock and all!

Our schedule was basically like the one we had followed in the minor seminary. Morning prayers and a half-hour of meditation in the large wood-paneled prayer hall preceded Mass, after which we had breakfast and then studied.

The particular form of meditation or mental prayer that we followed at St. Patrick's was that of our Sulpician tutors, in the spirit of their great founder, Father Olier.

The Sulpician method, designed like all the others to make one a more perfect follower of Christ, can best be summed up in the phrase: "Christ in my mind, in my heart and in my hands." Meditating on Our Lord's life each day was designed to lead us to converse intimately with Him, to become more like Him and ultimately to act in a way that would make us more worthy to be His representatives in the world.

At the end of meditation we recited this beautiful prayer in unison:

"O Jesus, living in Mary, come and live in Thy servants, in the spirit of Thy holiness, in the fulness of Thy power, in the truth of Thy virtues, in the perfection of Thy ways, in the communion of Thy mysteries: rule over every adverse power by Thy Spirit to the glory of the Father. Amen."

The seminary's daily routine had a few "breaks." Each Wednesday we could leave the grounds and take a walk in the beautiful California countryside. Sunday was special, too, because we could have visitors. My parents, brothers or sisters or some of my relatives, came about every second week. They brought the latest family news and, invariably, a box of candy or home-baked cookies which were always happily received. During the week, visiting priests often came to speak on a variety of specialized subjects.

I had been much impressed by Father Price and the three other Maryknollers who had stopped off at St. Patrick's during the previous year on their way to China. And now, early in my first year in the major seminary, Father James A. Walsh, the other co-founder of Maryknoll, came to talk to us.

My interest in this missionary society had grown during the previous year. I had become a regular reader of *The Field Afar*, and as a result, knew much more about the organization and the men in it.

At the time Maryknoll was founded in 1911, there were scarcely fifteen American Catholic priests in mission lands, which is easily explained by the fact that the United States itself was considered a missionary country until 1908. European Catholics were widely represented in this field, as were American Protestants. It was largely through Maryknoll that American Catholics took the first important step in this essential function of the Church.

When Father Walsh spoke to us on that fall day in 1919, I remember how he emphasized particularly that the faith, hope and charity of America could—and should—be sent abroad.

He was one of the most important and enthusiastic pioneers in this field. And although the Maryknoll Fathers were still limited in numbers, their earliest missioners were already at work abroad. There was much work to be done before they could make the impact he envisioned, but the future of the movement, as he saw it, was bright.

Americans, he insisted, should be going in greater numbers to missionary lands. Europe had already accomplished a great deal, but it had suffered much from the tragedy and destruction of World War I. As a result, we in America had not only the opportunity and the privilege, but also the obligation, before God, to make our own contribution.

After Father Walsh left, my fervor for mission work grew

steadily and I read each copy of *The Field Afar* with increasing attention. Not too much time passed before I spoke to Father Jean Ouvrard, my spiritual director, about my feelings for Maryknoll. But this French Sulpician Father, who was always bright, gay and enthusiastic, neither encouraged nor discouraged me: it was a matter I had to decide for myself. So, a year later, when I heard that Father Walsh was coming to St. Patrick's again, I decided to ask him if I could join Maryknoll.

During this second visit, in the fall of 1920, Father Walsh reported on the progress of his missioners in South China. He described in some detail the growth of Maryknoll and the seminary at Ossining, New York. Its enrollment was still below a hundred students then, but its spacious grounds included a large farmhouse and a couple of smaller buildings.

When I asked if I could talk with him, he agreed at once. As the time for the appointment came, I went up to the second-floor guest room. He was busy at his desk as I entered, but he stopped what he was doing, welcomed me gently, and beckoned me to a chair.

Almost before I knew it, I lost my uncertainty and found myself telling him of my enthusiasm for Maryknoll work. His comments were sincere and understanding. When I asked what steps I might take to transfer to Maryknoll, he told me that I could send for an application without further authority. But after that I would have to get permission from my parents, my superiors at St. Patrick's and, above all, from the Archbishop of San Francisco.

I tackled my parents first. I was skeptical about how they would respond to my new determination to leave California for New York and then for some far-off pagan village in the Orient.

"What's wrong with you?" I was asked when I made my first tentative approach during one of their visits to the seminary. "Can't you settle down in one place and stay there?"

Their attitude didn't surprise me much and I couldn't really blame them. Because of the lack of a foreign mission tradition in the United States, they were little prepared for this new proposal.

Reluctant as they were at first, I bided my time and finally they relented. I had explained as gently as I could that, though I very much wanted their approval, I felt I must go to Maryknoll with or without it. They knew I would be twenty-one in just a few months and free to make my own decisions.

When I spoke to the rector of the seminary, Father Ayrhinac, he was very gracious, as always, and gave me every encouragement. He explained that I would have his approval but pointed out that the actual permission would have to come from Archbishop Hanna of San Francisco.

By then it was the spring of 1921, and the end of my second year in the major seminary. If I was to make my move, now was the time. So when I heard that Archbishop Hanna had scheduled a visit to St. Patrick's, I hurried to the rector to explain what I had in mind and to ask him for an opportunity to speak to the archbishop. Now I remember very little of his visit, except for the fact that he spoke to the student body in the study hall. The only thing on my mind was going over what I would say and what I thought he would say.

As he left the study hall, the rector gave me the nod to come and be presented to the archbishop.

I don't know how well or badly I said what I had rehearsed for the previous hour, but Archbishop Hanna listened with kind attention.

"You may go, my son, with my blessing," he told me, nodding slightly as he spoke. "And you may return," he added just as pleasantly, "any time you like."

It was as simple as that. And, as it turned out, the whole process had been much easier than I had thought possible.

Though the worst was over, many details were still hanging fire. My parents had agreed verbally, but now I had to get their approval in writing, as well as a letter from the archbishop confirming what he had told me. I also had to have a written recommendation from the rector of the major seminary, a report of my standing in my classes, and a doctor's certificate.

Though all of these were assured, it took some time to bring them together. It was almost the end of the term before I finally sent my application off to Maryknoll with all that had to accompany it. Then the only thing left to do was to sit back and wait.

After what seemed an endless period of time, the term was finally over, and each of us stored our books and other belongings in preparation for the long summer vacation. We took off our cassocks and birettas and donned the black suits, the white shirts and the black hats and ties we wore when away from the seminary. Then the whole body of seminarians took off for home.

I didn't expect to leave for New York—if accepted by Maryknoll—until August at the earliest. But I couldn't seem to settle down or make any plans for the summer until I heard from Father Walsh.

Fortunately for my peace of mind (and for my family, who probably got tired of my fidgeting around the house), I didn't have long to wait. During June, right after my twenty-first birthday, word reached me that my application had been approved and that I was to begin my studies at Maryknoll in September.

I had left most of my belongings at St. Patrick's, and even though it would be two months or more before I had to send them East, I couldn't wait. I hurried down to Menlo Park to pack up all my books and other treasures and shipped them off to Maryknoll on the spot.

In August, after a fast and scarcely remembered summer, I

bought my ticket East and, with plenty of time to spare, left Oakland on my first trip across the country.

Until now I had never been outside my native state. Except for the region about San Francisco Bay, I had seen little even of California. I decided to buy a ticket over the Western Pacific, the Denver and Rio Grande, the Burlington, and the Baltimore and Ohio, so that I could see at least a little of the country on my way to Maryknoll.

With ten days to spare, I stopped at Salt Lake City, Chicago, Washington and New York.

I've always been glad I took that route. The four completely unique cities, each with its own unusual history, tempo, and physical appearance, gave me at least a little insight into the varied and fascinating nature of this wonderful country and the people who live in it.

On the way, I caught glimpses of other cities and towns, and breathtaking views of canyons, mountains, and almost unbelievably extensive plains. For the young homebody on his first real trip, the experience had a fairy-tale quality about it that even my future travels in various parts of the world could never quite match. For the first time in my life I had a real sense of this land that was mine.

New York was my last stop before Maryknoll. Knowing that I would have many other opportunities to explore this fascinating city, I decided to tour it in a once-over-lightly fashion which included the first-time thrill of a subway ride, the sight of Times Square, the Battery, the Hudson River, as well as the bustling activity of the waterfront, with the big ocean liners coming and going. Then I took a train to Ossining and a taxi to Maryknoll.

I thought I knew what to expect. After all, I had been reading *The Field Afar* for several years and had heard Father Walsh describe the place. But what I had read and heard and imagined did not equal what I saw. California has many areas of striking and almost unsurpassed beauty, but even with this background I was unprepared for the breathtaking sweep of the lower Hudson River Valley—the Palisades, the wide-spreading reaches of the Tappan Zee, and the green, rounded hills of Westchester County.

I was especially struck by the view of the countryside as the taxi climbed a curving road four or five hundred feet above the sparkling Hudson. A fieldstone wall covered with vines ran along beside the road as we turned through a simple gateway. And then I saw a big frame farmhouse just ahead.

The taxi stopped near the foot of a flight of wide steps leading up to a huge, homey-looking porch.

"Maryknoll!" said the taxi driver over his shoulder, and as I stepped from the car and turned to pick up my suitcase, three Maryknoll students came hurrying down the steps and welcomed me warmly.

CHAPTER V

PREPARING FOR A MISSION

Ten years before I hopped out of that taxi at Maryknoll, the establishment of a Catholic foreign-mission seminary in this country was considered improbable to nearly everybody but the two priests who succeeded in doing it.

Even by 1921, there was little to look at. But the unpretentious farmhouse that was "the seminary" and the other smaller buildings told only a small part of the story.

Maryknoll was far more than buildings. Its distinguishing mark, above all else, was its joyous apostolic spirit. It was a gaiety that got into the blood of any newcomer as soon as he arrived.

Under the inspiring direction of Father James A. Walsh, the Society had twenty priests and sixty-five students by 1921. While we never had to endure any unusual hardships, there were enough inconveniences, especially at first, to remind us that our goal was the foreign missions.

In those days, the Maryknoll seminary was more rough-hewn than most, simply because it was scarcely out of the incubation stage.

When I first arrived on the scene, there were five buildings and one under construction.

The erstwhile farmhouse where the taxi had deposited me was called "Rosary House," and as Maryknoll's central building, it included the chapel, an office for Father Walsh, a couple of classrooms, a kitchen, dining room and living quarters for students on the upper floors.

A large, somewhat rambling tenant house down on one corner of the grounds had been fixed up for the Maryknoll Sisters, and was known as St. Theresa's.

A converted carriage house and stable—St. Michael's—housed the Maryknoll Brothers, and another renovated barn called St. Joseph's provided small rooms for twenty-five or thirty seminarians.

The offices of *The Field Afar* had the distinction of occupying the only new building—a two-story fieldstone edifice.

The unfinished seminary dominated the landscape then as it does now. It was partially covered by a temporary roof and, even in that state, fifteen or twenty seminarians called it home.

During those early years, as the Society expanded, the buildings "changed hands" from time to time. When we students were all able to move into the partially completed seminary, Rosary House became the temporary motherhouse for the Sisters, and when they moved on, the Brothers inherited it. It still serves as their headquarters.

The Brothers worked side by side with the Maryknoll priests, multiplying their effectiveness by relieving them of many chores and freeing them to do the priestly work that would otherwise be impossible. Besides receiving a solid spiritual foundation, the Brothers were trained in mechanics, electricity, carpentry, printing and other skills that would aid the over-all work of the Society in winning souls to Christ.

What was true then is still true today. In the fields afar, the Brothers supervise the erection of missionary buildings, help to teach better farming methods, supervise medical dispensaries, direct boys' clubs and instruct in mechanical arts and crafts. On the home front, they help maintain the houses of training and take care of those tasks that are essential to the smooth running of any institution.

The Maryknoll Sisters were originally an auxiliary group to the organization created by Fathers Walsh and Price. But in 1920, a decree from Rome established them as an independent community. By the time I arrived a year later, the first group of twenty-five Sisters, under Mother Mary Joseph, their foundress, had pronounced their vows, and another fifteen were readying for the step.

The rapid growth of vocations to their community soon called for larger quarters than the various buildings on the seminary grounds could provide. They bought property across the road and, by 1932, had built a motherhouse which is still the headquarters of the some sixteen hundred Maryknoll Sisters. They are, by far, the largest group of American women in the Catholic foreign missions. Besides staffing their own far-flung works, they are closely associated with Maryknoll Fathers in Asia, Africa and Latin America, as well as at the Maryknoll center, just as they were when I was there as a seminarian.

At the time of my arrival on the scene, the Brothers didn't completely fill St. Michael's, so the seminarians used one small room for a classroom and some of us lived on the second floor. It was here, after I had been received by Father Patrick Byrne, the seminary's spiritual director, that I was assigned a nook. A couple of months later, I was moved into an equally simple but slightly bigger room in St. Joseph's, which stood some hundred yards to the west of St. Michael's and across a curving, tree-lined lane.

From the time Maryknoll came into existence, *The Field Afar* played a very important part in the organization's development and growth. Founded and for many years edited by Father Walsh himself, this monthly magazine presented the aims and progress of the mission cause to subscribers all over the United States. It also stimulated the moral and financial support so vital to Maryknoll's development. The magazine was so important that the first entirely new building at Maryknoll was erected to house its offices. Though printed elsewhere, the magazine was edited here and addressed and prepared for mailing by a staff of Maryknoll Sisters.

This was Maryknoll as I came to know it in the weeks that followed my arrival in September 1921.

Though classwork didn't start for several days, the seminary's schedule was already in effect. We arose at five-thirty and attended meditation and Mass before breakfast. Then came a Maryknoll specialty—"morning duties." Mine was to sweep the big front porch. (Shades of porch-cleaning days at home!—except that this one was fully seventy-five feet long and ten feet deep.) Others had similar jobs—dusting, cleaning, dishwashing, making up a priest's room, and other domestic chores. The process was so well organized and efficient that it took only about fifteen minutes each morning to get the whole place in apple-pie order.

Manual labor was also part of the daily routine. We usually spent an hour at it, and on holidays much longer. Though neither the Brothers nor we seminarians took part in any of the new construction that was always going on, we tried our hands at almost everything else. The Brothers actually did the lion's share of the work, and we took on the fringe jobs, such as washing windows and polishing floors. We worked in the garden, too, and most of us came to be reasonably adept as carpenters when simple tasks had to be done.

With a half-dozen wooden structures to keep in good condition, there was always plenty of painting to do. We developed a knack with things mechanical and electrical—at least some of us. I was never expert at any of this myself.

The farm, with its three or four teams of horses and about thirty or forty dairy cows, was pretty much the Maryknoll Brothers' preserve, though we did help occasionally.

Heavy and long as this work often was, it gave us a feeling

of participation that our classwork couldn't provide. A gratifying sense of accomplishment and of proprietorship went hand-in-hand with jobs well done—as when the steps that led up to the porch had to be replaced, or the cupola on the seminary roof repainted.

We knew, too, that it was all part of our preparation for the really rigorous conditions of missionary life in foreign lands.

By the time a week had passed and our classes started, I had fairly well settled into place.

Father Walsh was the mainspring of the seminary. Though he did not teach a specific class, his influence permeated everything. He presided at all the seminary's spiritual functions—at morning, noon and evening prayers. At other times during the day, he was readily available and, though an exceedingly busy man, was always easy to approach.

After dinner and supper each day, he took his "stand" in the hall outside the dining room, waiting for those who wished to see him. There was often a long line, and I can still see his sturdy figure as he listened thoughtfully to those of us who had come for advice or information, or who hoped to obtain his permission to do this or that.

He was remarkably keen and invariably perceptive and understanding. He always appeared to be looking beyond his immediate surroundings to the big world, and it was probably this great apostolic vision that gave him such a remarkable sense of balance, just as his quiet humor helped him to keep things in proportion.

We seminarians seldom left the vicinity. We were permitted off the grounds one day a week and, during each summer, we were allowed a month's vacation. On our "days off" we usually walked or rode bicycles together and, in the course of time, got a pretty good eyeful of the countryside for several miles around. New York City, about thirty miles from Maryknoll, was far outside our normal radius. "New York Days," however, did come a couple of times a year and we went in the morning, spent the day there as we pleased, and returned in the evening.

Of the ten or twelve priests who made up the teaching staff at the seminary, only Father Leopold Tibesar was a product of Maryknoll. The seriousness and zeal of this young red-haired priest from Illinois made a lasting impression on those of us who attended his class in dogmatic theology.

Father Lydon, a secular priest who was "on loan" to Maryknoll, taught canon law and moral theology, and did both unusually well. The short, stocky Irishman spoke with a slight brogue and never let his considerable scholarship get in the way of his great and lighthearted sense of humor. He soon knew us all personally and had a very good idea not only of our individual capacities but also of our personal backgrounds.

I remember during one class when we were having a discussion about accidents, someone gave a figure for traffic deaths that seemed too high to me. With the idea of setting the matter straight, I made the remark that, for the period referred to, I believed such deaths had numbered only about two thousand.

Up went Father Lydon's eyebrows.

"*Only?*" he replied in a mild state of shock. "Only two thousand, you wild Westerner?"

Among our professors and instructors were three Dominicans who were also "on loan"—Fathers Callan, McHugh and Reilly. Father Reilly taught both philosophy and French, while Fathers Callan and McHugh, who were co-editors of the respected *Homiletic and Pastoral Review*, taught Scripture and theology.

During our first year we studied fundamental and moral theology, Sacred Scripture, ecclesiastical history, sacred eloquence and sacred music. In the summer we took up the philosophy of religious education and were given an introduction to linguistics. Thereafter came dogmatic theology and second- and third-year courses in moral theology, Sacred Scripture, Church history, liturgy, pastoral theology, canon law, and missiology.

In my second year at Maryknoll, I became the regulator, or "bell ringer." Bells were a big thing at Maryknoll. We literally lived by them. The man who rang them had to get up before everybody else and go to bed after the rest of the seminary had settled down. The system was electric and was controlled by a central button which I was to press at the appointed hour.

The night before my new job began I solemnly set, not one but two alarm clocks. The bells were due to ring at 5:30 A.M. and I, of course, had to be on my feet even earlier—I, who needed much more than a nudge to get up at the regular time!

My own treacherous timepiece got itself overwound and never went off at all. The one I borrowed apparently tinkled at 5:15, but so softly that I kept right on sleeping, blissful and untroubled, until ten minutes to six.

At that point, somebody—I never learned who—rang the bell and got the seminary off to a late start from which it never fully recovered that day. But the seminary's troubles seemed small compared to my own sense of inadequacy and abysmal failure. My big chance—and I threw it all away the first morning!

It was pretty grim going through the motions of work and classes and putting up with the jibes of my classmates. After lunch, I got in line to see Father Superior, as we called Father Walsh. Waiting until I was absolutely the last, I blurted out that I had overslept despite the precaution of two alarm clocks. Father Walsh tilted his head a little, smiled, and said softly— "I envy you!"

Throughout the three years I spent at Maryknoll, work

continued on the new fieldstone structure, a part of which had been temporarily roofed when I arrived. There was other construction, too, as there continued to be in the decades that followed.

Even the most casual visitor could notice the great efforts that were being made to ensure the permanence of the new seminary building. Its sturdy foundations and thick walls were just the beginning. Much more work was still ahead before its final size and shape were arrived at. In fact, it was another thirty years before its capstone was finally put in place and it appeared in its present form. It was evident that the time required to build it was less important in the eyes of Father Walsh than the excellence of its construction and the purpose it was to serve.

Today this particular building is by far the largest and most important structure at Maryknoll. It houses the administration offices of the worldwide operations of the Catholic Foreign Mission Society of America as well as the Maryknoll Seminary staff and students.

During my days in the seminary, some of us had a few construction plans of our own, though they weren't nearly as important or noble. One aspiration was to build a tennis court. The location we finally found on the west side of the unfinished seminary was good, but it was completely choked with lumber, fieldstone and rubble that had to be carted away. This dampened our ardor somewhat. But tennis was my favorite game, and several of the other students agreed that building a court was a fine idea.

Father Raymond A. Lane, who was then the rector, had no objection to our working on the project, so long as we did it on our recreation time and not as part of the regular manual-labor assignment.

This was not quite what we had hoped for, but we got busy on it anyway. With each passing day of work, the pile didn't seem to get much smaller. What did diminish was the number of volunteers who had enthusiastically joined in the project at first.

I myself was not too happy about having to devote all my recreation time over so long a period. But it was my brain-child, and perhaps sheer determination kept me at it. Besides actually working on the "project," I constantly had to drum up new workers to replace the ones who had thrown in the towel.

In time we cleared the surface of the debris. But to get a self-respecting court, we had to go down another ten inches and fill it in with a stone base and a deep covering of clay. Then it was necessary to level the surface as best we could with shovels, hoes and rakes. Next we had to roll it over and over again, filling in the hollows and cutting down the elevations. Finally, we were ready to erect our high backstops and place the posts in position. After months of "hard labor," our tennis court was finally finished! All we had to do now was mark out the lines and stretch the net.

The little group who had persevered from the beginning had every right to be proud. Now to take off our labor-stained clothes, and reappear in tennis togs to test out the fine new court with the proper dignity!

But it seemed that there were others with the same idea. Even before we started back to our rooms to get ready, four students clad in immaculate white ducks took over. As far as I can recall, not one of them had lifted a finger during "construction." Now, however, armed with rackets and balls, they faced each other across the net and began to play a very good game. They obviously enjoyed every moment of it, while we who had done all the work sat glumly and watched.

When I finally played my first game, I began to realize something that had never occurred to me before and that I have never forgotten since. In some very fundamental way, the successful completion of this often discouraging but self-imposed job taught me the importance of following through with any worthwhile task, regardless of the hardships involved or the lack of appreciation. This lesson has helped me over countless obstacles ever since.

School terms, even in the seminary, eventually came to an end. We were given a month's vacation each summer, but it was an expensive proposition to make the long cross-country trip home. So those of us who stayed at Maryknoll studied, worked and made a few forays into New York and occasionally went swimming at Croton Point.

One summer I was sent to St. Vincent's Hospital at Eleventh Street and Seventh Avenue in New York City, to study first aid and gain a little medical experience that might prove beneficial in future missionary work. At most of the outposts in those days there were few hospitals, doctors or nurses, so what I learned at St. Vincent's might prove very beneficial some day.

We had all attended the first aid lectures given by Dr. Paluel Flagg at Maryknoll, but St. Vincent's would add first-hand knowledge in helping the sick.

It was a rare experience. Few nonmedical people have a chance to see such a closeup of hospital practice. I toted trays, carried bedpans, learned to make hospital beds, went out on ambulance calls, served in the emergency room, and observed medical and surgical techniques.

In the process, at least a little practical knowledge rubbed off. It also gave me a new understanding and respect for the skills and extraordinary devotion of the Sisters, the doctors and the nursing staff.

As I visited among the patients and learned to listen to their troubles, a new appreciation dawned on me of Christ's meaning when He said: "I was sick and you visited me." There were times, I knew, when a troubled, fearful or pain-wracked man or woman would rather have had a sympathetic ear than anything else in the world.

My favorite "assignment" in the hospital was the children's ward. Even when it wasn't my regular duty for the day, I tried to stop by for a few minutes. The youngsters were always gay and appreciative and it really was a "tonic" even to be able to tell them a story or two. I used to go during nonvisiting hours, thinking they might be lonely and would like to see a new face. But inevitably I was the one who got the boost. Many of them were there as long as I was, but some came and went fairly quickly. Regardless of their length of stay or degree of sickness, however, they always seemed to take their burdens lightly. These short visits have always stood out in my mind as stimulating reminders that one who tries to help others in Christ's name usually gets far more than he gives.

Throughout my three years at Maryknoll, I had fully expected to remain there for the full four-year course.

Each time the newly ordained Maryknollers left on Departure Day for foreign lands, I became more anxious for the day to come when I, too, would be sent into the mission field. And as each passing year brought me closer to that time, I felt more deeply the urgent necessity of the work we were to do.

At the end of my third year, however, when the fourth-year men received their mission assignments, three of my classmates and I were surprised to find our names posted on the assignment sheet, too. We were to go to Catholic University in Washington, D.C., and I was to specialize in medieval history!

Just where this would lead me I didn't know, but I assumed that whatever work I was to do in the future would be aided by the courses I would take. So, in the autumn of 1924, I packed up my bags and headed for Washington.

CHAPTER VI

A PRIEST AT LAST

It was quite a shift of gears to go from the routine of Mary-knoll to the cosmopolitan atmosphere of Washington and the Catholic University.

Along with my studies in medieval history, I took the regular seminary courses that I would have pursued at Maryknoll. This meant a crowded schedule, but spending the little free time that was left became a welcome challenge.

I never did find out why that course in medieval history was chosen for me. It may have been that my superiors thought they might eventually assign me to teach in one of the Maryknoll seminaries. (They didn't, as it turned out.) Or it may have been that they wanted some of the seminarians to study under the brilliant man who taught this course— Monsignor Peter Guilday—known to the students simply as Dr. Guilday.

But whatever the reason, it was a distinct advantage to spend a year at the Catholic University of America. It had been founded in 1884 and had opened its graduate school of sacred sciences in 1889. Schools of philosophy, law and social sciences were added in 1895, and a school of canon law in 1923. When I arrived in 1924, the university, which had earned a well-deserved reputation, consisted of eight or ten buildings and had a student body of about a thousand.

Along with three Maryknoll priests and four other students,

I lived in a small house that had been rented for our use. It was only four blocks from the university, so we could get to and from classes in just a few minutes.

The course in medieval history stood out clearly among the other subjects. It covered an age which has puzzled, intrigued and inspired historians for centuries. Though marked by defects and excesses, this age also produced countless saints, unsurpassed works of art, magnificent cathedrals and intellectual greatness. Recent historians have attributed our modern political systems, our scientific thought and our art to the development of principles formulated during this period of vision, beauty and vigor in which the people succeeded remarkably well in blending the divine with human affairs.

Studying under Dr. Guilday was a rewarding experience. His distinctive touch made this era a fascinating and very human subject.

"Don't get too excited about facts and information," he told us. "You must know the facts, of course, but whenever any of them slip your mind you can always look them up again. The big thing is to get the meaning behind the facts."

Shortly after the start of the term I was assigned a thesis on the Latin Empire of Constantinople (from 1204 to 1261). With the tremendous facilities not only of the university library but also of the Library of Congress at my fingertips, I enthusiastically tackled my research at every free moment. I worked early and late, until I had amassed nearly fifteen thousand words on my subject. I was eager to finish it as soon as possible, so I could study theology and the other regular seminary subjects without the burden of an unfinished thesis on my mind. But I was a little overeager, as was evident from Dr. Guilday's attitude when I handed in my finished product before the school year was much more than half over.

I don't know how good that dissertation was, but Dr. Guilday made it perfectly clear that I had been very premature indeed to write my thesis so early in the game.

"This will never do," he told me as he gave back what I had so proudly handed in. It was with some humility that I started all over again. The second time, I was more careful and thorough and, thanks to Dr. Guilday, learned the value of the basic fundamental of all study and writing—research.

Although I learned many useful things that year, none has served me better in preparing *Christopher News Notes*, our syndicated newspaper column or our radio and television broadcasts than the ability to distill a few lines of writing from a mass of material. Sometimes, in preparing the *News Notes*, I gather, read and digest hundreds and even thousands of separate articles or items on a single subject before finally completing an issue.

The following spring I handed in another 15,000-word thesis. This time it was accepted, which meant that I was now qualified to receive my master of arts degree. Having also completed my seminary courses, I looked forward to being ordained shortly.

My year at Catholic University brought with it the great advantages of studying in the nation's capital. Contacts and associations of many kinds proved to be important in rounding out my education.

Except on Saturdays, when I was free to do pretty much as I pleased, classes, studies and religious duties accounted for most of my time. During the week I spent so many hours studying at the Library of Congress that I began to feel I had established squatter's rights there. But as I came and went, I grew familiar with the Capitol, the Supreme Court and other government buildings. Sometimes when Congress was in session and I had a little free time, I joined the tourists in the gallery of the Senate or the House of Representatives. On Saturdays I visited the city's museums and art galleries, trying to absorb the history and beauty of their vast collections. So, in a way, I attended two educational institutions that year— the Catholic University and the fascinating city of Washington.

During the spring of 1925, not long after the famous cherry trees blossomed, Archbishop Hanna of San Francisco arrived at Catholic University for the annual bishops' meeting. Remembering his kindness to me when I had asked to transfer to Maryknoll, I went to pay my respects. While we were talking, I told him about completing my studies at the University, and my plans to return to Maryknoll for ordination with my classmates.

"How about being ordained in San Francisco?" he asked.

The idea surprised me but it was certainly appealing. I would have to get permission from Maryknoll, which, the archbishop assured me, would most probably be granted. Then he added: "And if you want, I'll be happy to ordain you by yourself."

After proposing this equally unexpected idea, the archbishop continued in his typically generous way: "How about August fifteenth? The Feast of the Assumption. I'll ordain you any place you want . . . in the cathedral . . . in the chapel in my house . . . or, if you prefer, in the chapel of one of the hospitals."

At last my mind began to click. Since the archbishop was so gracious, I suddenly made a bold suggestion of my own.

"How about my parish church," I blurted out, "St. Francis de Sales in Oakland?"

Even as I asked, I realized that what I was proposing was almost unheard of.

"Fine, fine," he agreed. "What hour do you have in mind? Make it any time you want."

I was thinking rapidly by now. Usually, ordinations are held at nine or ten o'clock in the morning. But I knew that the congregation of St. Francis de Sales wouldn't be very big at those hours on a weekday. Most of my old friends attended an early Mass before going to work for the day. (Although this was to be a Saturday, they still would be working for a half-day.)

"Would seven-thirty in the morning be too early?" I asked.

"Fine. Fine," the archbishop replied. "I'll be there. You just write me the details."

When I left the archbishop, I went right home and wrote to Father Walsh telling him of the archbishop's gracious offer. He promptly gave full approval and told me that he would write the archbishop to that effect. Now that I had the green light from Maryknoll I could give Mother and Father the good news. I wrote an exuberant letter and got back an equally delighted one. Not only would my parents and brothers and sisters be spared a cross-country trip to attend my ordination, but all my uncles, aunts, cousins and friends could be there, too. Everyone, Mother wrote, was thrilled.

When my work was finally over and I had my new degree tightly rolled and packed in my belongings, I returned to Maryknoll for a few weeks and then took the train for California. Father, Mother and all the family met me at the Sixteenth Street station in Oakland. I remember how delighted I was to see that they were looking forward to the coming event with a joy equal to my own. All their hesitancies and doubts of the past were gone, now that "a priest in the family" was practically a reality.

After I got settled in at home, I went to see Monsignor Dempsey, the new pastor at St. Francis de Sales. I had previously written him about the plan Archbishop Hanna had proposed, and during our visit he confirmed the arrangements, including the idea of having the ordination at seven-thirty in the morning.

Saturday, August 15, the great Feast of Our Lady, dawned

bright and clear. I awakened with a feeling of lightheartedness and gratitude to God for all that this day meant; for Archbishop Hanna's goodness to me; and for the fact that I could be surrounded by my family, relatives and friends. One more joy was still to be added: a number of my former classmates at St. Patrick's, who had been ordained about two months earlier, also attended my ordination.

Each step and word at this solemn and symbolic ceremony carry a profound meaning. I vividly remember the voice and even the tonal quality of the archdeacon as he spoke in Latin: "Accedat qui ordinandus est ad ordinem presbyteratus." ("Let him who is to be ordained to the order of the priesthood come forward.")

Then followed the voice of the notary as he read my name and, once again, that of the archdeacon as he asked that I be ordained.

Wearing a plain alb—a long white linen garment, bound at the waist by a cincture—I approached the archbishop as he sat before the altar, and prostrated myself before him.

"Scis illum esse dignum?" ("Dost thou know him to be worthy?") I heard him ask and, when the archdeacon had replied, the centuries-old ritual began. The archbishop's address to the clergy and the people . . . his admonishment to me . . . the Litany of the Saints . . . the laying on of hands . . . the prayer.

Next came the placing of the stole and the chasuble upon my shoulders and the maniple upon my left arm. Another prayer followed, and a hymn, and, as I knelt before the archbishop, he anointed both my hands with holy oil. It is hard to capture in words my feelings during that ceremony. Joy and unworthiness were mixed as the archbishop pronounced the following words in Latin:

"Vouchsafe, O Lord, to consecrate and sanctify these hands by this unction and by our blessing.

"That whatsoever they shall bless may be blessed, and whatsoever they shall consecrate may be consecrated and sanctified, in the name of our Lord Jesus Christ.

"Receive power to offer sacrifice to God and to celebrate Mass, as well for the living as for the dead, in the name of the Lord."

Then, as the archbishop began the Mass, I as co-celebrant said it with him. I had become a priest!

After the ceremony, we all went back home for a family breakfast, which evolved into an all-day reception. Since we were a big family, there were many relatives and friends of all ages, and it was a joyful occasion from every aspect. Mother and Father had kept me up to date with family news while I was at the seminary. But that afternoon I caught up with friends that I hadn't seen in years and, between the reminiscences and reports on what everyone was doing "at work and home," it was a wonderful reunion. Thanks to Mother's gracious planning, it went on and on without a hitch.

The next day was another landmark—my first solemn Mass. It was a particular thrill to be able to give Holy Communion to my parents and my family—and at St. Francis de Sales, which had been the scene of so many important events in all of our lives.

After the Mass, Monsignor Dempsey gave a dinner for the priests who had come to be part of the two-day event. Among those who were there were many of my St. Patrick's classmates, and Father Joseph McCormack, who had been two years ahead of me at Maryknoll. At the time of my ordination, he was in charge of the Maryknoll promotion center in San Francisco, which also served as a stopping place for missioners in transit to and from the Orient.

When I had left Maryknoll, I had fully expected that it

would be a short visit home and that I would return to Catholic University for another year of study. But when I got to California, I received word to wait there for further instructions.

I was delighted to have a little extra time with my family, but it wasn't long before I received the news that I would be staying on the Coast—not on vacation, however. Father Walsh wrote to tell me that Father McCormack had been assigned to a new Maryknoll mission in Manchuria and that I was to take his place in San Francisco!

There was much about this new assignment that was both challenging and pleasant. San Francisco is an attractive city and, with my family just across the Bay in Oakland, I felt very much at home.

When I moved into the Maryknoll house, I found that I had inherited a smoothly running operation from Father McCormack. The house was an old residence at the corner of Vallejo and Fillmore Streets and, from it, the hillside slanted steeply down to San Francisco Bay, about a dozen blocks away. Remodeling had provided an office, a chapel and modest living quarters. Keeping it in order and looking after visitors proved to be no great problem, since a competent Maryknoll Brother was assigned to the house, too.

My other duties were left pretty much up to my own initiative. Basically, my job was to make the work of the Maryknoll Fathers better known, recruit students who wanted to be missioners, and gather funds for missionary work. This gave all sorts of scope for originality, so I knew that I had to keep my wits about me if I was to be successful.

Because our missioners were at work in Asia in growing numbers, the house in San Francisco was a beehive of activity with their coming and going.

Their first-hand accounts of Maryknoll's overseas activities were a great help to me as I tried to spread the story of the mission work.

In the fourteen years since the Society had been founded, it had become increasingly well known, and there were now many groups interested in what our missioners were doing. So I soon found myself speaking in churches and schools and before civic and fraternal groups about their work, their plans and their needs in "the fields afar."

At this time, construction was underway for a Maryknoll preparatory seminary at Los Altos, California, only ten miles or so from St. Patrick's Seminary at Menlo Park. Other preparatory seminaries had already been established by Maryknoll in the East, but this was the first on the Pacific Coast. The building was rapidly taking shape and, though all major decisions concerning it were still being made in New York, I was chosen to act as Maryknoll's representative until a rector for the new school was appointed. When it opened in 1926 under Father Henry A. Dirckx, I went back to full-time promotion work.

Fund-raising was entirely new to me. The ins and outs of undertaking an annual benefit card party at the Fairmont Hotel on Nob Hill, for instance, simply had to be learned as I went along. One lesson particularly stands out in my mind. It involved the seminary at Los Altos and the day I took one of my candy-store uncles, Walter Selby, down to see it.

Our thirty-five-mile drive down the peninsula from San Francisco was very pleasant, and my uncle was favorably impressed with the visit. As we started back to the city, it struck me that he might be willing to contribute to the building fund —and possibly in a fairly substantial way.

I was thinking in terms of $1,000 and didn't know whether to mention the specific sum or just ask if he would like to help.

The miles were clicking away while I weighed the pros and

cons of my approach and tried to keep up a pleasant conversation at the same time. Finally, I decided to ask point-blank if he would like to contribute.

"Sure," said Uncle Walter, "I'll be glad to—I'll give you a hundred dollars."

My hopes were a little dampened and after a few miles I decided to try again. So I asked if he wouldn't like to make it a thousand dollars.

"A thousand!" he repeated in a horrified voice, and with that, I suddenly felt as if I were all hung about with icicles. He went on in a way that left no doubt in my mind that my pursuit of the matter had not been well received.

Although there was a definite restraint in the air for the rest of the ride, he didn't withdraw his original offer, and I'm glad to say that despite my fund-raising "tactics," he didn't lose his interest in the work.

To this day, nearly thirty-eight years later, I still thank my uncle for the valuable lesson he taught me.

In the years that followed, I was almost constantly engaged in raising funds for the missions. But never again did I make a specific request when talking to potential contributors. The experience with my uncle convinced me that it was better, from every point of view, simply to make needs known and then leave it up to the individual to help or not as he wished. Far more is gained, I began to realize, when people contribute out of conviction rather than by pressure from anyone outside themselves.

Years later, this idea was carried into Christopher work. Over and over again, the value of people giving because they want to and not because they have been asked has been proved. This accounts for the policy of no memberships, dues or fund-raising drives which was to characterize the Christopher formula from its start.

In trying to dramatize the needs of Maryknoll missions and

thus encourage a wider interest and support for the men in "fields afar," I began to wonder just how much it actually cost to sustain a missioner in the field. I questioned returning missioners and tried to learn what I could from other sources. I found that, though every missioner could certainly have used far more, the basic bedrock minimum costs were as little as a dollar a day. The tragedy was that, for many missioners, even that was hard to come by.

As I gave my talks and tried to get support for Maryknoll's activities, I began to refer more and more often to this dollar-a-day need. I pointed out how helpful it would be if interested individuals would decide to support a missioner for one or more days each month. I made no specific requests and I carefully avoided obligating anyone to a particular sum or a special period of time. But to my great satisfaction, there were an increasing number of offers to help with monthly contributions that would defray per diem costs.

In making the "sponsor-a-missioner" idea known, I emphasized that anyone signing up should feel free to discontinue his help at any time; also, that any help given to Maryknoll should not interfere with personal or parish obligations.

I had no idea then what the future of this "sponsor" idea would be. I hoped that it would eventually be employed on a far wider scale and would become, by the grace of God, a source of continuing mission support, both for Maryknoll and other apostolic groups.

So began my first years as a Maryknoll priest—not *in* the mission fields as I had hoped, but at least working *for* them.

CHAPTER VII

A GLIMPSE OF THE ORIENT

A letter that opened a new chapter in my life arrived from Father Walsh in the spring of 1928. He wrote to say that within a few months a small group of priests would accompany Auxiliary Bishop John J. Dunn of New York to the Eucharistic Congress in Sydney, Australia, and take "the long way home" via a quick trip through Asia. Since Bishop Dunn was director of the Society for the Propagation of the Faith for the Archdiocese of New York, he wanted to see some of the mission work in the Far East.

But the wonderful personal news in the letter was that a recent contribution to Maryknoll had been earmarked to cover the round-trip passage of one of our priests—and the one chosen was myself.

Though I knew the necessity of the work I was doing, I had always wanted to go to the missions. This hurried visit to the South Pacific, Australia and Asia would far from fulfill that desire, but it would at least give me a chance to see a few aspects of missionary work.

My job at the San Francisco house was temporarily covered by Father Charles F. McCarthy, who was at that time also in charge of the Maryknoll Junior Seminary at Los Altos.

We left San Francisco in August aboard the Matson liner *Monterey* and made our way to Sydney via Hawaii, Samoa and the Fiji Islands. This was my first ocean voyage and I was a little nervous about it. As it turned out, I had good reason to be. Before we had so much as steamed out of the Golden Gate, I discovered that I was definitely not a sailor. I became very seasick and continued to be for most of the rest of the trip. No matter what the weather, I always felt at least a little queasy whenever we were at sea.

Our stops at the islands were short, but even a day was infinitely better than never getting there at all. I especially regretted not having enough time to visit the Kalaupapa leprosarium on Molokai in the Hawaiian Islands. In fact, of the eight principal islands, we saw only Oahu.

Like all tourists, I was struck by the beauty of the beaches, the tropical flowers and trees, the rugged mountain terrain and the pleasant climate. But when I visited one or two of the sugar cane and pineapple plantations and saw the people hard at work in the fields, I realized that this little paradise, so delightful to tourists, is not just a playground.

I also carried away with me the lasting impression that Hawaii was one of the few places in the world where such a unique amalgam of peoples—Hawaiian, Japanese, Chinese, Filipino and Caucasian—have learned to live together in harmony and mutual respect.

The island group of Samoa is another of the world's beauty spots, and here again we saw the Polynesian natives who are found mostly in Samoa, Tahiti, the Marquesas Islands, New Zealand and Tonga. They are tall, statuesque people with brown or olive skins and wavy dark hair. We were told that the Polynesians owned nearly all the land in the Samoan Islands and that the local government was by *matai*, or tribal chiefs.

Samoa was once called the Navigator's Islands because the Polynesians were the most expert of primitive navigators. Some day I would like to return with enough time to get to know these gentle, dignified and highly artistic people.

A Glimpse of the Orient

The people of the Fiji Islands, which was our next stop, are Melanesians and are thought to be a mixture of the Papuan race and either the Polynesians or the Malayans. I particularly remember one big and somewhat ferocious-looking islander. I was walking along Victoria Parade in the small attractive city of Suva on Viti Levi, the largest of the Fiji Islands.

My host was showing me the "rain trees," the Government House and the Botanical Gardens. His words were lost on me when this muscular six-footer came along. He was probably in his forties, with dark complexion, high cheekbones and the frizzy mop of hair that many Melanesians have. He must have weighed close to two hundred pounds.

My specialty at Catholic University had been medieval history, not Fijian, but I had picked up enough information to know that cannibalism had been no stranger to these islands as late as the 1870s.

"Look over there," I broke in with perhaps a touch of anxiety in my voice. "That big fellow looks as if he might have been a cannibal."

"That's right; he used to be," my companion said calmly.

He then went on to tell me that the man had long since been a Christian, and explained that the gradual reduction of cannibalism had been largely due to the zealous work of the French priests who had been missioners there for many decades.

Distances in the Pacific are hard to grasp. It is farther from San Francisco to Honolulu, for instance, than from New York to Panama, and by the time the *Monterey* had taken us to the Fiji Islands we had traveled as far as from Washington to Moscow.

As we sailed from Suva Harbor, we were still nearly two thousand miles from Sydney. But finally our ship picked up

her pilot outside the entrance to Port Jackson, steamed past
famous Sydney Heads, and landed at the beautifully situated
capital of New South Wales.

Sydney is the largest of all Australian cities. Approximately
half of all the island continent's people live in the forty-mile-
wide area that is known as Sydney Basin.

Because our party had come to Sydney for the Eucharistic
Congress, the week we spent there was mostly devoted to attending its solemn functions. But we did get a chance to see
some of the city and its suburbs. By the time we left for Singapore at the end of the Congress, we had been duly impressed
by the beauty of Sydney's harbor, its handsome churches, public buildings, and the broad and well-kept parks. It was hard
to believe that only a century and a half before, this modern,
bustling metropolis had been a nameless place on an almost
unknown continent.

While in Sydney, I visited with Mark Foy and his family,
owners of a big department store there. I had come to know
them during their visits to California, where they also had a
home. When I was leaving, they presented me with a generous purse for the missions and also a personal gift—a packet
of Mother Sills' pills for my seasickness! They recommended
that I take one just before sailing and another an hour later.

When we had been at sea just about an hour the steward
delivered a cable to me. It was from the Foys and read: "Time
for your second pill." Mother Sills did help, but I was still
not a first-class sailor.

Steaming up the east coast of Australia, our Dutch ship
paralleled the Great Australian Barrier Reef for twelve hundred miles, rounded Cape York, Australia's northernmost
point, and entered the Arafura Sea.

Off to the north, not far beyond the horizon, lay the giant
island of New Guinea, which is just now being thrust into
the modern world. Ahead of us, for another twenty-five hun-

dred miles or so, lay countless islands that then were known as the Dutch East Indies but today make up the independent nation of Indonesia.

We stopped for a few hours at Batavia, Java, now called Djakarta. I had been told that the Javanese are among the most progressive and cultured of all the Malayan peoples, so I wanted to know more about them. I decided to leave the other passengers to their hurried sightseeing and shopping and to spend my little time ashore where the natives were— in one of their marketplaces.

Knowing not a word of the language, I contented myself with picking my way back and forth among the milling crowds. They were pleasant people to be in the midst of— slightly built and brightly dressed. As I passed, many of them smiled a shy, silent greeting. I dodged scores of hurrying bicycles, paused to watch the vendors, and marveled at the way the barefoot women gracefully carried baskets of fruit, jars of water, freshly laundered clothes or various purchases on their heads.

In any marketplace of Europe or America, I would not have been particularly conspicuous, dressed in my clerical black. But there among the gaily clad, golden-skinned Javanese, I must have stood out like a magpie at a convention of birds of paradise. Unlike a magpie, though, I was made welcome again and again with those lovely smiles, and I couldn't help but be touched by the friendliness of these people whose beliefs, surroundings and training were so different from mine.

Later, on deck, I talked with a small group of fellow passengers about our time ashore. As I enthusiastically described my experience, one dignified American lady seemed a bit upset about the whole thing. Feeling her disapproval, I directed my remarks to her and enlarged still more on the delightful time I had had.

When I had finished she turned to an acquaintance who

sat beside her and remarked: "When *I* go to a new country, I don't waste my time in marketplaces or watching dirty people. I'd rather spend it seeing the beautiful homes and lovely gardens."

Though her remark disturbed me, I felt that little would be accomplished by taking issue with her then and there. She certainly meant no harm, yet her attitude hit at the very heart of the basic problem in the world today—the responsibility each of us has to fulfill the simple command of Christ to "Love one another as I have loved you." (John 15:12)

I knew that her attitude, which is typical of so many well-meaning people, could not be changed overnight. But I couldn't help thinking about it during the next few days as we made our way across the Java Sea towards Singapore. I kept coming back to the same old conclusion: that not much progress would be made in Christianizing the world until each follower of the Lord is helped to realize that the transformation of the world must start with him, and depends to no small extent on how he applies Christ's commandments to every facet of life.

From Batavia, our ship sailed north, passing between the tin-producing islands of Banka and Billiton and then among the islands that form a complicated cluster off the southern tip of the Malay Peninsula.

Those of us who were China-bound transferred to another ship at Singapore. Although this city was not founded until 1819, its fortunate location has made it one of the world's great seaports and, more recently, one of the important airports of the Far East.

Before sailing time, I decided to take a ricksha and see some of the sights. The man who pulled it was very friendly and spoke English quite well. Starting from the Raffles Hotel, he took me to see all of the city's commercial houses and then across the little river that penetrates the city near the government offices. Next came Victoria Memorial Hall, the supreme court, and the city hall, after which I began to lose touch with where we were.

We were going farther and farther from the business section. But I decided to let my guide do it his own way. Suddenly he stopped and gestured towards the top of a small hill. He pointed to a new shrine of the "Little Flower" and said: "She loved all people—everybody. And that is the reason for the shrine."

My guide knew little or nothing about Catholicism, but he had somehow realized that this monument had been erected there in Singapore to honor a girl who was interested in every human being the world over, even though she had lived and died in a cloistered convent in France.

It deeply impressed me to find that this ricksha man had been so caught by the childlike love of the Little Flower for all people that he wanted to bring it to others. In his own way, and really without knowing it, he was acting as a transmitter of the love and truth of Christ.

I couldn't help but think: if one man like this in faraway Singapore could take it upon himself to be a divine agent in his limited way, what great hope there would be for the world if countless millions, who are blessed with the fullness of Truth, would show similar apostolic imagination and initiative!

As we headed from Singapore to Hong Kong, we were at last approaching what I was so eager to see—the part of the Orient where the Maryknoll missioners had started their work. It had been only ten years since Fathers Price, Walsh, Ford and Meyer had arrived in South China. But great progress had been made, despite the fact that the Communists had been making strong attempts to entrench themselves.

During our short time in Hong Kong I stayed at the Maryknoll house, which served as a center for all our priests working in South China. Our visit was heightened because Bishop James E. Walsh was there at the same time. He was not only the first Maryknoll bishop but also the first American to be consecrated in China. When the announcement of his elevation had been made in 1927, he wrote Father General James A. Walsh: "The responsibility is mine, but the honor is Maryknoll's."

He had chosen Sancian Island for the ceremony. To any missioner, this spot held great significance as the scene of the death of China's first missioner, St. Francis Xavier.

Bishop Walsh followed in the steps of this illustrious predecessor. And, with the exception of the ten years he served as Superior General of Maryknoll, he has dedicated his life to the apostolate in the Orient. Even when the Communist threat became a reality, he chose to stay rather than return to the United States. He was determined to continue his missionary work no matter how much his efforts were curtailed. In 1958, the Reds gave him a formal prison sentence which practically assured that his life would finish among the Chinese people he had served for so long.

I was disappointed that the limited time in Hong Kong wouldn't permit us to travel into the interior and see our missioners at work. But one of our priests assured me that, "Even if you went a thousand miles into the interior, the villages you'd find would be pretty much the same as those ten or fifteen miles outside of Hong Kong."

Since I had time to see only one place, I settled on the leprosarium at Shek Lung, which is only about fifteen miles from Hong Kong near the railroad to Canton.

Since my knowledge of Chinese was nil, one of the missioners at the Maryknoll house in Hong Kong printed my destination in Chinese on a card, along with directions to be followed when I got off the train. I had learned one expression: "Tin jee po yau," which means "God bless you." With that and my printed instructions to fortify me, I took the train for Shek Lung, hoping to learn something not only of the leprosarium but also a little of China and its people.

At Shek Lung, I was startled to find that two hundred leprosy patients were being cared for by a single French priest and three Canadian nuns who served as nurses. The patients were in various stages of the disease, but most were able to help with the work of maintaining the place. Only the priest and the three nurses, however, were trained, and their hands were full.

As I was led through the sparsely equipped rooms, I saw with dismay the handicaps under which these four worked. At one point, a patient touched my arm and spoke to me. I couldn't understand what he was saying, but one of the nurses explained that he wanted to be my guide when I went to see the hospital's extreme cases. I heard him refer to me several times as "sen foo," which I learned was the equivalent of "father."

It was as "sen foo" that I was taken through a series of rooms where tragedy was etched on the bodies of the patients. In some cases the thickened and discolored flesh had formed great shapeless nodules. Some sufferers had legs and arms that were grossly misshapen, or "claw hands." Faces were sometimes so distorted that I could only guess what they had once looked like.

It made me heartsick to see so much suffering, and it was humbling to see the heroic charity of these dedicated missioners. Not only were they surrounded by sufferers from this ancient disease that most people choose to forget, but they were compelled to make the best of pitifully limited resources. Beds were merely straw-covered boards, and blankets were of burlap. There was no running water, and even medicines were in short supply.

In spite of all this the place was completely orderly and clean. Supernatural confidence and hope seemed to radiate almost visibly from the priest and the three nuns. More astonishing were the smiles on the patients' faces, even on those who had lost an eye, a nose or a cheek, or were otherwise grotesquely distorted.

A very old lady was in the last room we entered. As nearly as they knew she was eighty-three. I had been warned that she was in the last stages of the disease. She, in turn, had been told that a strange priest was coming—a new "sen foo" whom she had never seen.

As we went in, the wasted figure suddenly sat up, and before the nun could stop her, she was on her knees, and in a thin piping voice said: "Tin jee po yau, sen foo." "God bless you, Father." Then she asked for my blessing and in a trembling voice I gave it, my hands outstretched over her bowed head.

Her face, when I first saw it, seemed hardly to be a face at all, except for her eyes. The flesh on her hands had so thickened and discolored that they no longer seemed to be hands. Her body was shrunken, bent and gnarled. But her eyes were bright, and when I had given her my blessing, she looked up at me and smiled.

Never, I believe, have I seen a more remarkable sight. Where, a moment before, I had seen only the tragic remnant of a human being, I now saw, in that leprosy-eaten face, the beauty of a soul. I turned and left her then so that she couldn't see the tears that blurred my eyes.

The memory of that Chinese lady in the leprosarium has returned time and again to give my work added impetus and direction. Many times since, I have told her story, hoping that a description of the love and joy she radiated in the most disheartening circumstances would be a reminder to others of how they can reach out and share their spiritual wealth.

Shanghai was our next stop. At the time, it was one of the world's greatest seaports. No one who ever saw the Shanghai Bund, the embanked and busy street along a branch of the Yangtze Kiang, in the days before the Communists took control, could possibly have doubted the great commercial potentialities of China. Unlike Hong Kong, which was no more than a fishing village and a haven for pirates at the time the British took it over in 1841, Shanghai had been a city of importance since at least the 11th century. When it became a "treaty port" in 1842 its great commercial growth began.

By the time we arrived in 1928, it had attained astonishing proportions. It served as the "warehouse" for an enormous and immensely populous valley—the valley of the Yangtze Kiang. This, when connected with its subsidiary areas, includes more than half of China's four million square miles.

As in Singapore and Hong Kong, our time was limited and we had to be selective about what we were to see. I was able to visit a Catholic orphanage which was under the direction of a nun of the Sisters of Charity. Sister Elizabeth Praschma had been in Shanghai for sixteen years and, as it turned out, this daughter of the Count of Praschma of Haute Silesie was to spend thirty-nine years at that mission.

In discussing their work, she told me that members of the orphanage staff went out in the streets daily picking up abandoned infants that had been left to die in doorways and alleys about the city. Many of these could be brought to the orphanage and cared for—others were found too late. Sister Elizabeth told me that baptizing these pitiful little creatures be-

fore they died had been one of their regular—almost daily—
tasks.

"How many dying infants have you baptized over the
years?" I asked.

She shook her head.

"I don't know," she replied modestly.

"How many a year?" I asked. "Is there any estimate that
you can make?"

"I'm afraid I don't know," she repeated, but her mind was
busy. "Maybe," she said presently, "twelve or fifteen hundred
a year."

During the sixteen years she had been in Shanghai—or so
I figured—she had probably sent some twenty-five thousand
infants ahead of her to heaven.

Peking was our next destination. To reach it from Shanghai, we had to take a small coastal boat to Tientsin. In
good weather this was merely a two-day journey up the western coast through the Yellow Sea. The only trouble was that
the Yellow Sea was often rough and treacherous. I eyed the
small craft with a good deal of trepidation. It was manned
by a Chinese crew and an English captain.

"Will it be rough?" I asked him, a bit warily.

"I don't know," he replied. And then with a twinkle in his
eye, "I'm not planning to eat anything myself."

Fortunately for me, the sea was peaceful. A few days later
this same boat ran into such foul weather that it took five
days to make the trip that had taken us less than two.

As we sailed up the coast toward Tientsin, we passed the
city of Chefoo on the Shantung peninsula's north coast. Our
captain told us that this was where most of the American
hair nets were made. But in 1928, when American women
were bobbing their hair, the whole city and countryside had
come to an economic standstill.

From Tientsin, we went inland by car to Peking—a beautiful city despite its great poverty. I can still see its enormous red and violet walls, its ponderous Drum Tower and its sumptuous palaces. But the most impressive of its buildings was the Temple of Heaven, with its many colorful courtyards, its marble memorial archways and its majestic circular, open-air altar.

The altar seemed at least a hundred feet in diameter, and I was told that there was a special piece of marble in the center that only the emperor—when there was an emperor —was permitted to stand on when he came to worship the King of Heaven and Creator of the Universe, the one and only Person known to man who was admittedly greater than the emperor himself.

The colors in the temple were dazzling, and the glorious designs and splendid works of art testified to the philosophy of a great people. But the Temple of Heaven, along with so much else, has been forced, for the moment, to give way before the strangely un-Chinese doctrine of Karl Marx. But who can doubt that the King of Heaven, the Creator of the Universe, will ultimately prevail? Who can doubt that the people of China will throw aside this yoke and take the place in the world that their wisdom, practicality, great sense of beauty and spirituality have so obviously fitted them?

Returning to Tientsin from Peking, we took another small boat and sailed east over the Yellow Sea to Dairen in southern Manchuria. Again the weather favored us. During our brief visit there, we were invited to a Japanese home for dinner. The family members were good friends of the Maryknollers, and the red carpet was laid down in style for the American visitors. This festive Japanese meal included a selection of the choicest fish—served raw. I took one look at these "delicacies" and began to feel seasick again.

But despite my poor showing as a guest, the evening was delightful. The Japanese are charming hosts; they have exquisite manners and a keen sense of graciousness in putting guests at their ease.

We continued our way north until we reached Mukden, the capital of Manchuria, and the city from which the Mandarin dynasty had once ruled all China.

During a tour of the cathedral there, we learned a little about the hardships that come to that land in winter. In the sacristy, I was intrigued to see that the cruets used for the wine and water at Mass were kept in small rectangular metal containers. When I asked what they were for, I was told that "During the winter we have to pour hot water in those boxes so that the wine and the water won't freeze before Mass is over."

For similar reasons a small charcoal stove was often placed beside the chalice on the altar. One could only wonder what suffering the people of the region had to undergo during the cold winter.

From Mukden we headed south for Fushun—an industrial and mining center that then boasted the largest open-pit coal mine in the world. Here I was to have a closer look at Maryknoll missions. The area covered by our men was rugged and mountainous and about the size of New York State. In 1925, when Father Raymond A. Lane (later Bishop and Superior General of Maryknoll) established his headquarters at Fushun, there were some four million people in the district, about four thousand of whom were Catholics. By the time we arrived in 1928, a dozen priests covered the area, and a seminary was underway as well as schools and dispensaries. Maryknoll Sisters were not only conducting the regular work of their mission stations, but were also training Chinese girls who would be able to take over in case the Americans were forced to leave.

Though the thousands of miles we had covered on our trip had provided many opportunities for brief insights into mission life, this visit with Father Lane and some of the priests I had known during our years of training at the seminary brought home to me in a more personal way the challenges, difficulties and rewards of their endeavors.

A few further glimpses of Maryknoll work came on the next leg of our journey. As we headed down to Korea, Bishop Dunn's party was accompanied not only by Father Lane but also by Father Patrick Byrne, who had been rector of the seminary when I first entered Maryknoll. Since then he had pioneered the Society's work in Korea and was later to do the same in Japan. He was ultimately appointed Apostolic Delegate to Korea in 1949 and consecrated bishop. A year later he met his death at the hands of the Communists. At the time of our visit, we were able to stop at several of his missionary outposts and, here again, see some of the great headway being made.

One train ride during this part of our trip stands out in my memory. The railway car I had a seat in was filled with Chinese, Koreans and Japanese, few of whom seemed to possess much in the way of this world's goods. Except for the smiling Chinese vendor who sold his wares from a loaded basket, my fellow travelers had little to say. Most of them, swaying a little with the movements of the train, stared dully from the windows or tried to get comfortable enough to fall asleep.

When the vendor came my way, I spoke to him and was surprised to find that he not only spoke a little English but also was a Catholic.

He didn't talk to me much at first, but I kept watching him as he walked back and forth through our car. As he moved along the aisle and paused beside each passenger, I began to notice a strangely uniform series of actions and reactions. His pleasant and very mobile Chinese face would light up with a smile and he would make some remark that he obviously hoped would result in a sale. Occasionally he succeeded. Usually, though, the glum and sleepy passengers to whom he spoke responded only with a negative shake of the head. Then he would speak again, and sometimes this second remark brought a short, but very often none-too-friendly, reply.

As the vendor shifted his load a little and made ready to move on, he would make still a third remark. Surprisingly enough, this invariably caught the passenger's attention. Though they made no reply, they certainly looked up sharply, and they seemed much more wide awake and thoughtful after he had passed.

I saw this happen several times, and my curiosity got the better of me. What was this man saying that was so regularly answered first with but a silent shake of the head, second by no more than a gruffly spoken word or two, and third by such a clear expression of surprise and concern?

The next time he passed, I asked. Though his English was weak and my Chinese nonexistent, I finally understood his explanation.

He liked to talk with people, he told me, but most of the travelers were concerned with their own troubles and weren't very responsive. When he first approached a passenger he asked them what they wished to buy. Many were too poor to make a purchase. Still, even those who couldn't or didn't care to buy were sometimes willing to talk. In an effort to encourage them, he used his second question.

"Where are you going?" he would ask. Sometimes, a conversation would grow but most often they simply told him the name of the town they were bound for—Pyongyang, or Wonsan, or perhaps Seoul.

It was then that he would come up with his third question. "And what is that?" I inquired.

"I ask each person—where are you going when you die?"

This was more than amusing—it was amazing—and certainly gave me something to think about for the rest of that journey. The same sense of eternity that had done so much to lead me into the priesthood was startlingly crystallized on a dreary train ride through Korea. This vendor was a missioner in his own way. He wanted to do more than get to heaven himself—he wanted to help others get there, too. And he did it in the only way he could. If I had made the long journey to the Far East only to meet this one man, it would have been well worth it.

One more incident on that train ride is almost as memorable. I had bought some small, beautifully handmade rugs in Peking for the Los Altos seminary, and up to that point had carried them without mishap. But when I got off the train at Pusan at the tip of Korea, I discovered that I had left them behind. By the time I realized what I had done, the train had started back to Seoul, some two hundred miles away. I was due to take an overnight ferry to Shimonoseki, Japan, that evening, so I couldn't very well go chasing after them.

Rather hopelessly I reported my loss to the Pusan station agent. But he was reassuring cheerfulness itself.

"We'll phone the station at Seoul, report your loss and ask them to bring your rugs on the next run. They'll be here tonight before your boat leaves."

Though I didn't say so, I couldn't have been more doubtful. Even if somebody had not taken them home, how could I expect someone to search through the train for them and transfer them to the next Pusan-bound train? A lot of trouble for a stranger and his rugs.

But the rugs were at the station that evening, just as the agent had promised . . . an often-remembered lesson in honesty and efficiency.

In the three days following that eventful train trip through Korea, we made whirlwind stops at Shimonoseki, Osaka, Kyoto and Tokyo. There were no Maryknoll missioners in Japan then. But in our short stay we had an opportunity to see some of the work done by the French priests—many of whom had devoted forty to fifty years of their valiant lives to bring Christianity to the Japanese people.

Even in those three days we could not help but be captivated by this gemlike country with its charming terraced hillsides, beautiful gardens, rushing streams and waterfalls, and snow-capped Mount Fuji. The efficiency, neatness and graciousness of the people were evident everywhere—not only in their carefully planned gardens and houses, rice paddies and orchards, but also in every aspect of public life. For instance, their trains were always on time, and their engineers were immaculately uniformed and white-gloved.

Early in October we sailed from Yokohama aboard one of the President Line ships for the return trip across the Pacific. During the twelve-day voyage I had plenty of time to reflect on the simple but inspiring experiences of my brief visit to the Far East.

I was certainly determined to look for every possible opportunity to promote the missionary cause. But little did I realize then what a profound impact this trip would have, not only on my immediate work, but also on what I was to attempt in the years ahead.

CHAPTER VIII

FROM SAN FRANCISCO TO NEW YORK

Maryknoll work was forging ahead when I got back to San Francisco, thanks to the devoted efforts of Father McCarthy. I returned to it with a fuller realization of why the mission cause should be concerned with "all men" and the whole of life, and not be regarded as a mere appendage of the Church's other activities.

Thanks to the movie camera I had taken on my trip to the Orient, I had been able to bring back a convincing, if non-professional, record of a few of the things I had seen—mostly missioners and their work. I had also bought a short film, showing some of the destruction the Communists had wrought in the parts of China where they were then operating. After extensive editing, the combined presentation ran about a half-hour. Together, the two films were a startling contrast.

Every chance I got, I showed them and, in a brief talk afterwards, tried to stress how important it was for each of us to show greater zeal, vision, daring and self-sacrifice for Christ than those working against Him displayed.

I pointed out that the Communists instilled a sense of personal mission in each of their followers and impressed on them that they could have a hand in shaping the world according to their philosophy of life.

Then I added that, while the Communists had no commission to go to the world with their strange beliefs, they were doing so on a frightening scale. Christ, on the other hand, did tell each of his followers to think, pray and work in terms of the "whole world" and everybody in it.

Each time I touched on this idea of personal responsibility, it seemed to strike a new and more responsive chord in the audience. People would listen attentively to a talk on missionary work and were very willing to contribute financially if they could. But I found they would react far more favorably when they realized that they could be missioners themselves by spreading the missionary concept to others and promoting the good ideas they believed in.

The idea of self-participation seemed to fill a gap in explaining the mission cause. It was not developed or refined at this stage, but the basic concept proved appealing and challenging.

The new reaction was exemplified in a graphic way by a young woman who came up after one of the talks and said: "This is the first time in my life that I have really understood what the missionary side of our church is all about. I always thought that all that was expected of me was just to give a little money. Until you pointed out how seriously the Communists take their cause, I never realized that I have much more than a financial obligation."

In the late summer of 1929, I attended the first General Chapter of the Society at Maryknoll's headquarters in Ossining, New York. About two dozen delegates were present for the meetings, which covered every phase of Maryknoll's work both at home and in the mission fields.

Before returning to California, I reported to Father Walsh on some of the promising developments that had been made possible as a result of the San Francisco center. I expressed the hope that we might eventually have many others like it across the country—an idea that, no doubt, he was thinking of long before it occurred to me.

Father Walsh reacted immediately to our conversation and instructed me to stop in Cincinnati on my way West. Maryknoll had a new preparatory seminary there on the grounds of St. Gregory's Junior Archdiocesan Seminary, and so there were possibilities for a San Francisco-type setup.

This side arrangement presented exciting prospects. I firmly believed that American Catholics had a tremendous missionary potential that was scarcely tapped. The Cincinnati endeavor could be a valuable opportunity to prove the worth of pursuing this idea on a broader scale.

Father Walsh and the late Archbishop John T. McNicholas of Cincinnati were good friends, so I received a warm welcome from His Excellency. His encouragement meant a great deal as I set about establishing the little office from which the work of Maryknoll might be made known and supported.

I just wanted to get the office started and make a few plans for the future on this first visit, since I had to get back to San Francisco and pick up work there.

I stayed a little longer than expected, however, thanks to my appendix. I had only been in the city about two or three days and was having dinner with some priest friends when it became apparent that I wasn't feeling in top form. I didn't feel drastically ill, so I did not mention it until we were on our way home, and then suggested that we might stop off at Good Samaritan Hospital. After a quick examination, the doctor said that it would be advisable to have my appendix out the next morning.

Having spent one summer at St. Vincent's, I had picked up some bits and pieces of knowledge about surgical procedures and so asked the doctor when I reached the operating room the next morning if he was going to give me gas or ether as an anesthetic. "Neither," he answered, "we're going to try a local on you." This is common practice today, but then it was rather unusual and a somewhat odd experience to be completely conscious and able to carry on a conversation the whole time. I remember asking the doctor, while I was stretched out on the operating table, when he was going to start cutting, and being told: "In a few minutes we'll have you all sewn up."

On the way downstairs, since I felt perfectly fine, I struck up a conversation with the nurse who was wheeling me back to my room and discovered that she had fallen away from the Church. So for the next ten minutes, we discussed the ins and outs of her problem. Then she reminded me that I had just had an operation and had better rest awhile. We continued the talk later with a happy outcome, I'm glad to say. The Lord often provides strange ways and means of doing His work!

Thanks to a quick recovery, I was out of the hospital in about a week and spent the next several days organizing the office and a schedule of talks for my next visit. Both clergy and laity were most helpful in lining up the opportunities to speak at churches and schools.

Arranging activities so I could travel between the two cities presented a few problems, but I managed to get back to Cincinnati in mid-March 1930 for a bit longer stay.

I had just about started on my prearranged schedule of talks and gotten the office under way when I received a telegram on April 6 that my father had died of a heart attack. This was the first great loss of my life and I felt it deeply.

That same day, Father Walsh happened to arrive in Cincinnati. When I told him the sad news, he generously gave me permission to go home. Naturally, my first impulse was to take off immediately and be whatever help I could to my mother and family.

So I telephoned Mother to discuss when and how I could get there. In those days, passenger planes were few and far between, and jets of course were unknown. I would have had to take a train for Chicago and then another for California. All of which would have taken just about four days. I would have gotten to Oakland barely in time for the funeral. The main disadvantage, from my point of view, was that all the time on the train would prevent me from doing the only meaningful thing I could for my father, which was offering Mass for him.

As Mother and I talked, we both began to feel it would be much better for me to stay in Cincinnati, where I could offer Mass for my father each day and carry on with the work in which he had become so very personally interested since my ordination.

My greatest consolation at the time was to remember how Father had constantly encouraged my activities and went so far as to accompany me on talks and help make arrangements for them. I never really doubted that he would have wanted me to do anything but stay on the job and offer the Holy Sacrifice for him each day following his death.

I was grateful that my sisters and brothers were with Mother, and I knew that it would not be long before I would be back on the Coast and able to be with them again. I felt I would probably be much more useful, particularly to Mother, a little later on. Father's death was a shock to all of us, of course, but it would leave a particular void in her life that would be even more difficult in the months following his death.

In November 1930, I was called back to Ossining for further discussions about the development of Maryknoll centers.

At the time, there was not one in New York City. Although some years earlier we had had a house on East Fifty-seventh Street, it was sold in 1925 and the proceeds used to buy our present Collegio Maryknoll on the Via Sardegna in Rome.

Plans to reopen in New York had been shelved to make

way for more pressing needs. But about this time, a good friend of Maryknoll—Miss Julia Ward—offered Father Walsh the use of a two-room office in the small building she owned at 16 East Forty-eighth Street, just off Fifth Avenue and two blocks from St. Patrick's Cathedral. Her offer happily coincided with my suggestion for a Maryknoll promotion center in the city. Father Walsh accepted Miss Ward's offer and delegated me to go ahead and open the office myself.

It was an unexpected change, but he who proposes ought to be prepared to dispose. So early in December I moved a desk, a few chairs, and a small cot into our new quarters. Then I went to San Francisco to wind up my affairs there and spend Christmas with my family. As it turned out, it was the last one I was able to have with them. I returned to New York in January 1931 to begin my new work.

While my assignment on the West Coast had included forays up and down California and inland to Denver, the dense Catholic population of the New York area was something to reckon with.

My territory included not only New York City itself, but also Long Island, northern New Jersey, and Westchester County. I was also expected to do what I could in Connecticut, Rhode Island and Massachusetts. This is a region in which more than ten per cent of all the people in the United States live. More important, it is one of the most influential areas in shaping the thought of our nation. As I looked around again at my nearly bare and utterly silent little office and tried to figure out where and how to begin, I wondered if I was not beyond my depth. In many ways, my task seemed almost impossible.

One of my first moves was to go over to St. Patrick's Cathedral and tell the priests there that I would be glad to help, if any need arose.

To my delight, they said they would be grateful if I would

"fill in" and say the seven o'clock Mass on the following Sunday morning.

I returned to my fifth-floor nook on Forty-eighth Street and tackled the many details involved in turning the bare rooms into an operating office. The smaller of the two rooms became my bedroom, while the larger served as the office. By the time I went to bed that Saturday evening, it looked as if things were beginning to fall into place. I wound my alarm clock, set it for 6:00 A.M., and promptly fell asleep.

The January sky was a little bright for comfort when I awoke the next morning. To my horror, I saw that the clock had stopped at 2:00 A.M. I grabbed my watch from the chair beside my cot, and discovered the awful truth—it was then 7:45—three-quarters of an hour after my scheduled Mass at the Cathedral.

"What a way to start in New York!" I thought. "And at the Cathedral, no less!"

My only hope was that my apology would be accepted. And the sooner I made it, the better. Dressing and shaving in a whirl of guilt and panic, I flew over to the cathedral to render an account of my miserable stewardship.

I would not have been surprised if the sacristan had been a little standoffish when I appeared. But to my relief, he was quite friendly. When I finished my apology he smiled and told me not to worry. He said that an out-of-town priest had arrived at about one minute of seven and he had said Mass in my place.

The schools and churches in New York City were so numerous that no single individual could speak at all of them. These, together with the extensive suburbs, gave me quite a bailiwick.

The range of my activities expanded more rapidly than I had thought possible. From Manhattan, I extended my work

into Brooklyn and gradually to churches and schools in
Queens, New Jersey and the Bronx. Now and then I ferried
over to Staten Island or took a train up to Westchester and
the adjacent areas of Connecticut.

As time progressed, I began traveling in eastern and northern Connecticut, as well as Rhode Island and Massachusetts.
By the second year, I was driving to Boston every Saturday,
speaking in a church there on Sunday, and driving back to be
at my desk the first thing Monday morning.

Gradually as I told the story of Maryknoll to so many different audiences, I began almost subconsciously to emphasize
not only what my listeners could do to assist missioners by
prayer and finances, but also how they could play a missionary
role themselves. I tried to impress on them that even if they
never boarded a ship for China or Africa, they had been sent
by the Lord to do some work that no one else could ever
accomplish. In trying to point out to my listeners that they
had potential as missioners in their own milieu, I seemed to
have finally found a way to add that new dimension to my
work—the lack of which had bothered me for so long.

"You" was the word and idea I stressed wherever I spoke.
"You, individually, have a mission in life to fulfill—a special
job to do. No matter how narrowly you may be circumscribed
—no matter how small your ability or your circle of acquaint-
ances—no matter how limited your knowledge or experience
—you can do something that no other person can do to shape
the world in which you live."

The idea that first stirred me in San Francisco began to
take shape, and I found that people began to sit up and take
notice when they realized they could exert their own personal
influence in ways other than sharing the contents of their
wallet.

By the autumn of 1932, after nearly two years in New York,
my office was humming with activity, and I was doing my

level best to cover not only the city but also its widespread suburbs.

About this time I accepted an invitation to speak at the Convent of the Sacred Heart in Noroton, Connecticut.

Noroton is an attractive residential community on Long Island Sound, about thirty-five miles from New York City. My audience that day was made up of about sixty-five girls of high school age, who were attending the convent's boarding school. Their ages ranged from fourteen to eighteen, and I had been told that they were from many parts of the country, though mostly from the East.

I didn't know any of the girls personally, but as I looked about before beginning my talk, it appeared to me that they were somewhat above average both economically and socially. Though few of them would probably end up actually working in "the fields afar," I somehow felt that any apostolic motivation I could give this particular group of girls might develop into something for the missions and for the world.

The talk I gave was basically the one I had been giving ever since I reached New York. Nothing was memorized, and I tried to state my case in terms that would especially appeal to the specific audience. This particular one was attentive and I had the feeling that they were really interested.

I told them of the work of the Maryknoll missioners in Asia and of the difficulties they had to face. I don't recall the exact words I used or the instances I cited, but as I talked with them I tried to stress that each girl sitting there could personally do something, with the help of Christ, to shape the world for the better.

"No matter what your individual circumstances and surroundings may be," I said in effect, "you—you individually —can leave the world better for your having been in it."

I made it clear that I was naturally interested in any help that they might give for Maryknoll in Asia, but I also assured them that I was perhaps even more deeply concerned with what each of them could do throughout their lives as individual "Christophers." I reminded them that the word "Christopher" came from the Greek term *Christophoros*, meaning "Christbearer."

How I happened to use that word at that particular time, I don't know. To the best of my recollection I had never used it in that way before. But having done so, I felt that here, at last, was the root of the idea that had been in my mind for so long.

When I left Noroton that day, I had little notion of where this idea might lead. One of the girls who afterwards sent me a letter was probably not aware of it either. But six years later, she wrote from Baltimore to say that although she had long since forgotten everything else I said that day at Noroton, she had never forgotten my message that she, personally and individually, could be a Christopher or Christbearer.

And one reason her letter so greatly interested me was that I had not forgotten either.

CHAPTER IX

A LIGHT IN THE DARKNESS

In 1933, four years after "setting up shop" in New York, a friend suggested that a benefit concert in the Metropolitan Opera House would be a good way to raise funds for the missionary work of Maryknoll. This proposal involved a big undertaking for a novice like myself. The opera house, with its 3,336 seats, was such a massive place to fill that I was awed just thinking about it. But the idea seemed worthwhile, so I accepted the challenge and the results produced more than financial dividends.

The first step was an appointment with Earle Lewis, then assistant manager of the "Met," to discuss the project. It was in the morning, so instead of scores of well-dressed men and bejeweled women, the famous lobby was empty. Even the few electric lights seemed pale and feeble.

Mr. Lewis appeared promptly and efficiently outlined the terms that would govern the benefit we had in mind. It would be up to us, he told me, to dispose of the tickets ourselves. I must admit that selling over 3,300 tickets sounded like an enormous task. But my confidence grew when Mr. Lewis spoke with obvious understanding of such matters, and told me about many other benefits that had been most successful.

Then he suggested that we go into the auditorium and take a look at the layout. When all the lights are on and the house is filled, the Metropolitan is most impressive. The profusion of red and gold, the great expanse of seats, the tiers of boxes and galleries and the lofty ceiling can take one's breath away. As we entered, however, not a single light was on. I could vaguely make out Mr. Lewis beside me, but nothing beyond that.

"Dark, isn't it?" he remarked. "Wait here a minute, and I'll throw on the lights."

He disappeared down the darkened aisle. I waited. Then suddenly, far up on the stage, a single flame pierced the darkness. Mr. Lewis had lighted a match to avoid stumbling over a piece of scenery.

The sight of that tiny flame made an indelible impression on me.

Insignificant as it was, it was greater than all the darkness. All that was needed to banish the darkness completely was to multiply that flicker of light.

In a moment, the manager did just that. Crossing the stage, he turned on all the switches. In that instant, the darkness was gone and the opera house was flooded with light.

This little experience dramatized the old Chinese proverb that I liked so much: "It is better to light one candle than to curse the darkness." In a human way it echoed the divine advice of St. Paul to be daringly constructive rather than merely negative or critical: "Be not overcome by evil, but overcome evil with good." (Romans 12:21)

It was not long before Mr. Lewis and I worked out the details for the benefit at the "Met," and when it was held a couple of months later, it turned out successfully, as did later ones.

As time went on, I became increasingly engrossed in my work. Even though I couldn't be in "the fields afar" myself, I knew that our little New York office was doing more and more to help the missions.

In 1934, the Holy See appointed Father Walsh a bishop in recognition of his work in stirring up so many American

Catholics to the cause of the missions. His wish was to be consecrated in Rome, and it was my privilege to accompany him.

We sailed on the *Mauretania* and landed at Cherbourg. From there we took the boat train for Paris. For some reason, I felt at home as soon as I set foot in the city.

Paris, as my guidebook indicated, was originally known as Lutetia—a walled and fortified little island in the Seine, and the stronghold of a Gallic tribe called the Parisii. Eventually these tribesmen connected their island to both banks of the Seine with two wooden bridges. The original ones have been replaced many times in the centuries that have passed, but there are still two bridges crossing the Seine at these exact places—the Pont Notre Dame and the Petit Pont.

Only a stone's throw to the east of the island roadway that once connected the first two wooden bridges stands the Cathedral of Notre Dame.

Eight centuries have passed since this magnificent edifice in honor of Our Lady was begun in 1163. So it was with a good deal of awe that I approached it. I had seen churches in many parts of the world, but here for the first time I saw the model so many had imitated. As I gazed at this Gothic master-piece, I thought of the vision of its planners and the artistry of its divinely inspired builders and wished that I might have known those who had so successfully drawn men's hearts upward to the contemplation of God's majesty. I was re-minded of a little story I had once heard and have told many times since. It concerns three laborers working on a cathedral.

The first man was a glum-looking fellow. It was his job to cut the blocks of stone. "If I didn't have to earn a living for myself and my family, I'd quit in a minute," he used to say.

The second man's job was to cut the timber. He went about his work in a listless, grumbling fashion.

The third laborer possessed none of the manual skills of

the other two. He simply carried the stone and wood they prepared. But he sang and whistled as he trudged back and forth with heavy loads.

One day a passer-by beckoned to the third man and asked him what he was doing.

"What am I doing?" exclaimed the laborer in astonishment. "Why, can't you see? I'm building a cathedral!"

As I feasted my eyes on the massive power and serenity of the cathedral and recalled this meaningful anecdote, my mind made one of those "association" jumps. How wonderful, I thought, if thousands upon thousands of persons could somehow be inspired to play a part—even a very small one—in bringing God's beauty, love and truth into every phase of our modern life—just as that legendary laborer had in the construction of a beautiful cathedral.

After a few days in the French capital, we boarded an express train for Rome, the city that had been the center of the civilized world when Paris had been only a tiny barbaric stronghold in the Seine.

Our schedule in Rome was naturally centered around Father Walsh's consecration as bishop. He chose June 29 for the ceremony. It was the Feast of Sts. Peter and Paul and the twenty-second anniversary of the day he and Father Price had received approval in Rome to start the work that his elevation was recognizing in such a significant way.

It was a day that pulled many threads together. As we gathered for the ceremony in the chapel of the Propaganda College (the Pontifical seminary that trained priests for mission lands), the bells of Rome were ringing in commemoration of the city's heroes, Sts. Peter and Paul. Cardinal Fumansoni-Biondi, who headed the Church's mission work, presided as Consecrator and was assisted by two old friends of Bishop Walsh's—Archbishop McNicholas of Cincinnati and Bishop Dunn of New York. Among those on the altar were seminarians from the Maryknoll missions in China, Korea and Japan. The mingling of many nations in a universal ceremony was once again a strong reminder of the cause of Christ that should bring all men together.

During the two weeks we were in Rome, I was fortunate in having a great deal of free time to explore the city on my own, and I did my best to become acquainted not only with modern Rome but also with the monuments and sections that linked it with the past.

Naturally, my first visit in the Eternal City was to St. Peter's. I had seen many pictures of the great basilica, the curving Bernini colonnade that encloses the great piazza, the ancient Egyptian obelisk that marks its center, and the fountains to the right and left. But though, for a moment, these caught my eye, it was St. Peter's itself, just beyond them, which riveted my attention. The sheer grandeur of its tremendous dome and the heroic figures of Christ and the Apostles on the elevated parapet of its façade made me feel somewhat like a pebble at the foot of a mountain.

There, just beyond the Piazza San Pietro, the tortured martyrs of Nero's day had died "under the leadership," an inscription reads, "of the Apostle Peter." There, too, Constantine the Great, having ended the era of persecution in 313 A.D., built the first basilica above St. Peter's grave. In the course of centuries, many of the world's great figures have visited the successors of St. Peter. As I made my way across the piazza and through one of the great doorways of that vast church, I had never been so clearly conscious of the greatness of the Church and the privilege of playing even a small part in fulfilling Christ's command to "teach all nations."

I was fortunate to be included in a small group accompanying Bishop Walsh when he had a private audience with Pope Pius XI in his study. Bishop Walsh and the Holy Father spoke for a few minutes through an interpreter while the rest of us looked on. Whatever I might say about this heroic spiritual leader would be just a pale portrait of a man who, just a few years later, proved to be such a bulwark of quiet strength to a war-torn, frightened world.

It was obvious even then that he was deeply troubled by the rising force of Nazism. Yet in spite of the tremendous burdens he carried, the Pope took a sincere interest in everyone he met. In a semi-private audience I attended later, he walked slowly around the horseshoe-shaped line of pilgrims. An interpreter identified each person, usually by the country he came from. The Holy Father would say a word or two to each, frequently in the visitor's own tongue. I went with a New York group to one of these audiences and stood at the end of the line. When the interpreter presented me by saying: "Here is a priest from Maryknoll," the Pope's face lit up.

"Ah, Maryknoll!" he said, smiling at me. I will never forget how he somehow managed to make each person there feel especially honored and blessed—a rare gift in itself.

Several visits to the catacombs and to the ruins of the Colosseum were also part of that memorable visit to Rome. Those silent reminders of the courageous early Christians added still another dimension to the ideas that were gradually taking shape in my mind.

As an insignificant and even hated minority, they proved that even against discouraging odds, the most inconspicuous person can bring Christ's love, light and goodness to the world.

Historians estimate that eighty per cent of the early Christians were ordinary rank-and-file workers. Yet during the persecutions of the Church in the first centuries, these tutors, secretaries, nurses and laborers took their faith to their masters and even into the imperial household.

They realized that the message of Christ belonged to all, even their persecutors, and so, in the face of almost insurmountable obstacles, they found ways to serve as His instruments and to weave the principles of Christianity into the texture of pagan Roman life. Neither prisons nor persecutions could restrain their enthusiasm.

In a glorious manner, they overcame what must have been a strong temptation to stay hidden in the catacombs and care for their own private spiritual needs. As practical Christbearers, they realized the importance of bringing Him into the heart of the marketplace and sharing His love with countless others to whom the Redeemer was sending it through them.

As I prayed in the catacombs and stood in the Colosseum where these early Christians were thrown to the lions, my thoughts again turned to the staggering contribution that could be made by modern Christians, if they could be stirred to imitate the same vigorous zeal and apostolic resourcefulness.

While we were in Rome, I met some friends who were driving through Europe. Since a little over two weeks remained before Bishop Walsh and those of us who made up his party were to sail for home from Genoa, my friends urged me to join them in visiting Florence and Venice.

It was a rare opportunity and I am glad I was able to take advantage of it. I'll never forget the almost unequaled art galleries of Florence or the magnificence of Venice, with its Cathedral of St. Mark, its palaces, canals and fabulous history.

After my friends went on their way to the Italian lakes, I still had about a week before sailing time, so I decided to make my annual retreat at Assisi.

As I look back on those quiet days of recollection and prayer, I realize what a unique blessing it was to spend them in the place from which St. Francis rejuvenated so many phases of the world of his day.

Even in just a few days at Assisi, one could not help but

absorb some of the Christlike joy and determination that led
this apostle of the thirteenth century to bring the love and
truth of Christ to individuals in every walk of life.

As one old chronicler put it—the whole world found refuge
in the heart of St. Francis. The poor, the sick, the oppressed
and the fallen were special objects of his solicitude. The
tremendous capacity he had for practical sympathy gradually
warmed even the coldest and hardest individuals. His efforts
to alleviate human misery were after the mind of Christ, and
he tried to instill this same divine quality in each of his
followers.

He was more interested in providing solutions than in con-
demning or criticizing shortcomings. Rather than keep religion aloof from human affairs, he ardently strove to incarnate
spiritual principles into a world that he knew would perish
without them.

My retreat over, I left the peaceful Umbrian countryside
and rejoined Bishop Walsh and his group in the busy port
city of Genoa. We sailed for home on the *Rex*.

Nine days later I was back in New York.

Some time before I had left for Europe, the Forty-eighth
Street building in which my office had been located for almost
four years had changed hands, so we found new quarters in
an office building at 103 Park Avenue, on the corner of Forty-
first Street. The space was about the same and we settled in
quickly.

As it turned out, I was in and out more than I planned.
Early in 1934, the Society for the Propagation of the Faith
asked Bishop Walsh if I could be released on a part-time basis
to work as assistant to Monsignor William Quinn, the national director.

My main job was to prepare the Society's magazine, *Catholic Missions*. I felt we would win more friends for the mission
cause if we featured short articles, heightened by pictures, in-

stead of long stories. They spoke with a force and reality that could never be equaled by words alone.

Doing the preparatory work, which often included going through as many as a thousand photos and an almost equal number of letters and reports from the missionary lands, kept me on my toes. I tried to give readers a sense of belonging to the great missionary work of the Church, and to help them feel like personal participants and not merely financial "backers." All this was given more impetus and meaning because, at the same time, I had to carry on the responsibilities connected with our Maryknoll office in New York.

On April 14, 1937, during my second year of work for the Society for the Propagation of the Faith, Bishop James Anthony Walsh died.

His death marked the end of the first era in Maryknoll's history, and for those of us who had been privileged to be around him during his years as Father General, it was a deep personal loss.

Tributes to him as a priest and a leader came not only from those within his own Society but also from others far removed.

His place as co-founder of Maryknoll testifies to his idealism and vision. The years he served as general of the young society are obvious examples of his ability as a dynamic organizer with the courage of conviction and the simplicity of an abiding faith.

Perhaps one of the most satisfactory ways for me to recall the great debt I owe to him is to cite some of the counsels he continually stressed and that inevitably "rubbed off" to some degree on all of us.

His life's aim and purpose were clearly summed up in one paragraph of the last letter he wrote to present and future Maryknollers: "Our work is His work and you will make no mistake if you look to Him for guidance. All that He seeks from you is generosity and ready willingness to use the opportunities—or meet the difficulties which will inevitably present themselves."

He explained the meaning of Christ's command to "teach all nations" with vision and practicality when he said to us: "To work for Christ is a great privilege. To labor with Him, and in Him and through Him, mindful always that we are His willing instruments, is the assurance of our success, spiritual especially and often material."

The fullness of the missionary spirit, of which he was such an extraordinary example, accounted in no small way for the foundation of the Christopher movement. Its ultimate aim has always been to encourage the followers of Christ to integrate His love and truth into the vital fields of influence that have gradually gone pagan because they have been largely abandoned to those who do not know Him or who persistently spread hatred of God.

The missionary zeal that Bishop Walsh strove to instill in each of us was given a unique emphasis in one of his favorite expressions: "It is better to wear out than rust out." This quality of action came out in his own personal life—he never wasted a moment and, whether on a trip or at home, he planned every day down to the last minute. This often led those of us who were his traveling companions to have a few harrowing moments.

This attention to detail that ran through all his activities has never failed to impress and help me through the years. He felt very strongly that "big enterprises will fail if details are not watched." Often when I heard him stress this point I couldn't help but remember the similar advice my uncles had given me years before at the candy store—though for somewhat different reasons.

In one of his spiritual conferences to the seminarians,

Bishop Walsh brought this point out in another respect when he said: "He [Christ] wished to have it brought down through the ages that wastefulness is sinful. There is much to be done, so much material needed in life, that it is well to consider this matter. It is well for us to study the idea and watch over waste."

The proper use of time and talent was always an important consideration, and he was quick to advise: "To be busy is good but not enough; we need efficiency in God's work."

In considering any financial undertakings, he cautioned that: "We are stewards of the Master's goods and should keep this idea always before us. What is given up by the people outside . . . is for the cause we represent and I say that morally we have no call to it. It is given for the work and is to be used carefully. If we waste it, Almighty God may withhold much from us."

In the years that I was doing Maryknoll work, as well as in furthering the Christopher movement, these words of advice have had a special significance. I have always tried to practice a sensible economy and efficiency that would allow the highest percentage of each gift to go right to work and not be bogged down in overhead.

In the area of finances, the training and emphasis Bishop Walsh gave us on the importance of saying "Thank you" and the example he gave in immediately acknowledging correspondence have helped give wings to many an apostolic project.

Anyone who came in contact with Bishop Walsh couldn't help but have the feeling that he was interested in them personally. When we were seminarians, he used to address us once a week and give a report on the Society at home and abroad. He wanted everyone to feel a distinct part of all aspects of the work.

His whole life was powered by a burning love of God and

people, and he never missed an opportunity to encourage any individual he came in contact with to reach out with his faith and sanctify the whole of life. He showed an especially tender solicitude for persons who were not Catholics and, in turn, he was beloved by them.

Because he was conscious of the importance of the individual, he never overlooked the value of learning from others. He would tell us, "Don't stop suggesting simply because former suggestions have not been adopted." He once told Maryknollers: "I cannot urge you too strongly to be humble. The self-opinionated person accomplishes little and is a disturbing influence. Try to see the other person's point of view and remember that arguments, unless sincerely employed to get at the truth, are of little or no use." The oft-repeated suggestion in Christopher literature to "disagree without being disagreeable" could well be an outgrowth of this early advice.

Bishop Walsh had a knack of encouraging those who had even a spark of initiative, and he constantly reminded us to keep our eyes on future accomplishments and not to worry about past failures. He often said: "I never worry. I believe that we are doing God's work and that if we do our part, He will do the rest." This certainly has meant a great deal through the years, as has the example of his lightheartedness, which is such a needed and valuable ally in any apostolic work.

The motto which Bishop Walsh chose when he was consecrated in Rome in 1933—"Primum Regnum Dei" (Seek first the kingdom of God)—is perhaps the summation of his life and the heart of the examples and teachings he gave to each of us. In advising members of the Society he once said: "I have no fear for the future if Maryknollers, in all their actions and discussions, will forget self and keep in mind the will and glory of God."

Those of us who had the privilege of living with and being

trained under Bishop James Anthony Walsh will probably never realize fully how much we gained from this personal contact.

Since it was my good fortune to accompany him not only on the visit to Rome but also on many trips to various parts of this country, I could not help but pick up many valuable pointers that have bolstered my efforts ever since. Whatever success the Christopher movement has had, under God, is certainly due in no small measure to his dynamic apostolic ideas.

Bishop Walsh was deeply convinced that the missionary work overseas would never hit a big stride until the vast majority of Catholics understood and became personally involved in the universal mission of the Church.

The sense of eternity that pervaded his whole life, in an unusually joyful manner, left an indelible mark on me. He thought, prayed, talked and acted like a person who was hurrying on his way to heaven and wished to bring along with him as many people as he could reach.

In that final letter he wrote to all Maryknollers, he put this attitude in a nutshell when he bade us farewell, as he put it, "until we meet merrily in heaven."

CHAPTER X

THE CHRISTOPHER MOVEMENT GETS UNDERWAY

As the activities of Maryknoll grew, it became obvious that I couldn't do two jobs at once, so in 1937 I had to give up my temporary work at the Society for the Propagation of the Faith. By 1938 the small quarters we had been using for Maryknoll activities at 103 Park Avenue had become such a tight squeeze that we were authorized to buy a brownstone house at 121 East Thirty-ninth Street. It not only provided space for a larger staff but also a few rooms for Maryknoll priests passing through New York.

Many of these men were in transit to and from the missions. Our men had been at work in Asia for more than twenty years and, though their numbers were still small, the stories of their labors, especially in the early years of World War II, could not help but impress anyone who heard them. As I listened to one after the other, I became more and more convinced that their heroic experiences should be told to a big audience. I felt they would not only stimulate more Americans to follow in their footsteps but also might induce innumerable others to "lift up their eyes" and see the important contribution they could make by fulfilling the particular mission God had entrusted to each of them.

With this in mind, I tried to write down what some of the returning missioners told me. I never got beyond about four pages, but I was so struck with the importance of putting these stories in print that I talked about the idea at every opportunity. As a result, someone mentioned the possibility of a book to two literary agents—Helen Rich and the late Gertrude Algase. They talked it over with Mr. Charles Scribner, the publisher, and then came to see me. But when they asked me to go ahead, I had to protest that, while I had done some writing, I had never written a book, and couldn't begin to do the stories justice.

"I feel like a person who wants to give his friends a good dinner," I explained. "I know what they would like to have, but I can't cook well enough. It's the same with this book. I know many stories that should be told. But I can't write them as they should be written."

My visitors, however, were not to be put off.

"Suppose," they asked me, "we got you the best cook in town? How about Meyer Berger of the New York *Times?*"

They made it hard to say no, so I agreed to talk with him about the project.

A few days later, Mr. Berger dropped in to see me and I showed him the four pages I had written.

He read them carefully, and then glanced up.

"With stories like these," he said with characteristic generosity, "you don't need anyone to help you."

But I prevailed upon him to make up for what I lacked. And so I went to work with one of the most highly respected and admired feature writers in the newspaper field.

At various meetings in the next six months, we went over the material. He did most of the writing, but working in close association with him gave me wonderful practical experience. His insistence on detail certainly left its mark. I remember that the setting for one story involved a bush on the side of the road. When I first told it, I simply said there was a bush on the side of the road. But that didn't satisfy Mr.

Berger. He asked: "What kind? How big? What color? Was it dusty?" As I filled in the answers, the bush I had casually cited almost took on a personality. The details added the color and life that made the difference between a flat statement and an easily identified scene.

Thanks to his time and talent, Scribner's published *Men of Maryknoll* in the fall of 1943.

Mike Todd, the late theatrical producer, seriously considered a play based on *Men of Maryknoll*. In the end, it was decided otherwise, but while it was under consideration, Harriet Kaplan, Mr. Todd's secretary, read the book.

"These missioners," she remarked when she had finished, "are Christians with guts. There ought to be a million more like them."

There it was again—the dynamism of the missionary idea! I was convinced that if only it could be implanted in the minds and hearts of others, there would be far less temptation to drift into agnosticism, atheism, secularism or communism.

The United States, at that time, had a population of about 140,000,000, but approximately 100,000,000 men and women (and the total is even greater now) practiced no formal religion and were becoming less and less conscious of the great fundamentals of our Judeo-Christian heritage that make possible the blessings we all cherish.

This steady, dangerous trend towards godlessness was certainly a threat to the survival of our country as a free nation, and could well stifle the missionary work that Maryknoll was striving to do. It seemed to me that failure to nurture a personal sense of mission in more followers of the Lord was an invitation to spiritual disaster both at home and abroad.

And so, with World War II battering the peoples of many nations, I continued with more seriousness than ever to advance the simple apostolic idea that had urged me on for a decade and a half. Bishop James Edward Walsh, Maryknoll's Superior General from 1936 to 1946 (following the death of the co-founder, Bishop James Anthony Walsh), generously left all of his priests free to use whatever means we could to promote apostolic ideas, provided such efforts were based on sound principles and did not interfere with our particular duties. But in the early experiments with the Christopher idea, neither he nor any of us had any idea that the seeds being planted were soon to blossom.

As the war was ending, I wrote an article entitled "What About the Hundred Million?" In it, I urged the formation of a movement to "work out formulas of approach and techniques that could be used to advantage in leavening the marketplace." Then I came up with the phrase I had first used thirteen years before, when I spoke to that group of girls in Noroton, Connecticut. I wrote: "A possible name for such a movement might be 'The Christophers,' since all those connected with the movement would be, in a very literal sense, 'bearers of Christ.'"

I showed the finished article to Father John Considine, one of Maryknoll's best writers. He was always most sympathetic to every effort to spread the missionary idea and was particularly aware of the influence and the "lasting quality" of the written word. At his suggestion, I sent the article to the *American Ecclesiastical Review*. Its appearance in this publication, in May 1945, started a new chain of events that hastened the day for the start of the Christophers.

Countless letters and inquiries arrived, along with many requests for talks. As the Christopher idea began to take shape as a reality, I was reminded of that inscription on the walls of the Library of Congress that had deeply impressed me so many years before:

"For a web begun God will supply the thread."

Specific efforts to develop the Christopher idea had to be postponed, however, because during that same month of May 1945, Maryknoll work took me to California for a few weeks of mission talks. As it happened, it was fortunate because the events of that summer added new impetus to my gradually crystallizing ideas. My first stop on the Coast was San Francisco.

The representatives of forty-six nations were meeting there at the time to organize and prepare a charter for the United Nations. News of this latest experiment in international cooperation filled the daily papers. As I went about my own business, I became increasingly conscious of the enormous strength and vigor of those sent by the Soviet Union. Even the way they came and went about the city plainly suggested that they had big plans and were clearly aware of how important these plans were in shaping the future of the world towards Communism.

These representatives seemed to typify what little I knew about the kind of training militant Marxists are given— training which convinces each follower that he is part of a gigantic and almost irresistible force. Once that idea is firmly implanted by their Communist leaders, they work hard and well at any small assignment they may be given. They realize that whatever they may be doing is advancing the cause of worldwide revolution.

There is an impious kind of inspiration in Communism as it is taught today. In a deceptively clever way, it is using an idea about personal responsibility that has its roots in the Gospels. Even in this prostituted form, it has proved to be a powerful influence. How much more powerful would the true Gospel message be if it were spread as widely and effectively by those with Christian backgrounds!

I was glad to be on the West Coast again for another reason. It had been a long time since I had had an oppor-

tunity to see Mother and my brothers and sisters and their
families. Mother was now in her early seventies and, though
I didn't know it that spring, it would be our last visit together.
She died on January 3, 1946, after a prolonged illness. As
with my father, it has always been a consolation to remember
the great personal interest she always took in all the projects
in which I became involved. I credit her prayers in heaven
for much of the success with which our work has been
blessed.

My work that summer also took me to Los Angeles and
what turned out to be another decisive factor in the evolve-
ment of the Christophers. While I was there, an impressive
wartime pageant was staged at the vast Coliseum on Sunday
evening, June 10. More than 100,000 people were in the
audience.

Thanks to the magic of Hollywood, the arena had been
transformed into a realistic battle scene. Exploding land
mines shook the earth. Batteries of tanks roared across the
stadium. A mass formation of B-29s swooped down over
the watching throng. The noise was deafening, and the
overpowering effect emphasized the helplessness and insig-
nificance of the human individual in the face of such warlike
might.

But then something strange and unexpected happened.
The deafening uproar came to an end, and the master of
ceremonies stepped to the microphone and began to speak
to the listening multitude.

"Perhaps," he said, "you sometimes say to yourself, 'My
job isn't important because it's such a little job.' But you're
wrong. The most obscure person can be very important. Anyone here can exert a far-reaching power if he wants to do so.
Let me show you what I mean."

Abruptly, the lights that had brightened every corner of

the huge Coliseum were turned off. From almost daylight brightness the great arena was suddenly plunged into total darkness. Then the speaker struck a match and the tiny flame could be seen by everyone.

"Now," he went on, "you can see the importance of one little light." Then he added: "Now suppose we *all* strike a light!"

From every corner of the stadium came the sound of matches being struck and, faster than it takes to tell, nearly one hundred thousand pinpoints of light suddenly glowed in the summer night.

This was a dramatic repeat performance of that morning in 1933—twelve years before—when Earle Lewis lighted a match on the darkened stage of the Metropolitan Opera House. That evening in Los Angeles was another vivid illustration of the Chinese proverb: "It is better to light one candle than to curse the darkness."

As the vast throng left the Coliseum a little later, many must have given some thought to how much easier it would be to bring peace, and even happiness, to a heartsick world— if only enough people would combat the darkness of error by spreading the light of truth.

This experience strengthened my conviction that there would be high hope for a real and lasting peace once a sufficient number of people recognized that falsehood is the absence of truth in the same way that darkness is the absence of light, and hate the absence of love.

The Coliseum incident seemed too good to let slip by. I felt that it was a very strong illustration of the idea I had tried to promote in "What About the Hundred Million?" Before too many of the details slipped my mind, I decided to write it up for use in my promotion work later on. I was working on it one day at the Maryknoll house in Los Angeles when one of the volunteers who worked there offered to help type my notes.

The volunteer was Miss Florence Okazaki, who at that time was studying at the University of Southern California and spending a few hours each week helping at Maryknoll.

Since she was familiar with missionary work, she was sympathetic to the idea I was trying to get across in telling the Coliseum story. She caught the apostolic flavor right away and made some very good suggestions both on the writing and possible distribution of it.

Her alert, bright and generous outlook was a big asset and I told her that in the further development of the Christopher idea there would be a great need for people like herself. Any apostolic work depends to a large extent on whether those connected with it see the far-flung possibilities in such relatively simple operations as preparing the Coliseum story. Anyone who has the initiative to follow through on any and all angles adds a much needed and really indispensable plus to any job.

The day I was leaving California, Florence happened to be working at the Maryknoll house again. When I was saying good-bye and "thanks again" for her help, she said: "Don't forget to let me know if you ever need some help for the Christophers."

When I got back to New York in June, I found that many more letters, cards and requests for talks had piled up in response to "What About the Hundred Million?" This new evidence of interest convinced me that it was a case of "strike while the iron is hot."

Little by little, I began to work out some plans for starting a Christopher movement. I still hoped that whatever I might do would be simply the ground work for someone else, since I was thoroughly involved in my regular Maryknoll work and any other undertaking would have to be a side issue.

In pulling my ideas together, I felt it was particularly important to keep the Christopher movement simple—there should be no formal organization whatever, no memberships, no meetings and no dues.

The reason for this somewhat unusual formula was to focus attention on personal responsibility which, as I saw it, should be the fundamental idea. When a person realizes that God has delegated him individually with a special mission in life—a mission for which he alone is personally responsible—that person is more likely to go ahead on his own and do what he has to do.

Just how to launch this simple idea was the next question. No funds were available, except some unsolicited contributions that had come in. The first of these arrived from some of those who had read "What About the Hundred Million?" In January 1946, when *The Catholic World* published another of my articles, called "You Can Be a Christopher!" a few more voluntary gifts came in. This second article, though shorter than the first, attracted much more attention—so much, in fact, that I decided there really was a chance for the movement to succeed.

"You Can Be a Christopher!" was not profound. It merely repeated what had often been said before. I outlined "the Role of a Christopher" and followed with a few short anecdotes of how persons sparked by the Christopher idea had already made themselves effective. I ended it with the following observations:

For the next twenty or thirty years, maybe longer, this nation will play the leading role in world affairs. Which way will it lead the world? . . .
The answer is in our hands and in the hands of people like us. It is a terrible challenge. But we must face the facts. There is no

other way than the way of Christ. "I am the Way and the Truth and the Life." (John 14:6) If we but strike a spark, that spark, in the Providence of God, may burst into flame.

But there is no time to lose. We must show speed. The efforts of even the least among us can be blessed with results that will exceed the fondest hopes of anyone. God is behind us. He will supply His grace in abundance. It may be the most unusual opportunity in history to recapture the world for Christ. It is a great time to live.

During the time of preparation and since the movement has been underway, I have tried never to lose sight of what I regarded as the big objective behind the Christopher idea: to make every person a missioner. That, I firmly believed, was a goal that had to be reached if our foreign mission effort was to develop its full potential.

During the summer of 1946, Bishop Raymond Lane was elected Superior General of Maryknoll, succeeding Bishop James Edward Walsh. Since the Christopher movement had begun to show such promise, I asked Bishop Lane for permission to develop it on a more thorough basis. He liked the aim and informal setup and, like myself, felt that if the idea caught on, it could be beneficial in laying the groundwork for a greater expansion of missionary work in foreign lands.

Bishop Lane not only allowed me to devote as much time as I needed to put the movement on a solid footing but he also took a fatherly interest in all the planning. He always asked about the day-to-day details of progress and he was invariably pleased with the warm reception that the Christopher idea received from the very outset.

There are always lots of hurdles to get over in the first stages of any work, so his encouragement was a great boost.

The formal launching of the Christophers was not a very complicated affair. Since Bishop Lane graciously allowed me to use some space at the Maryknoll house on Thirty-ninth Street, it simply involved arranging some desks and engaging a few competent workers.

When it came to competent workers, my first thought was of the volunteer in California who had been so interested and generous in offering to help with an undertaking like the Christophers. I wrote to tell her that the idea seemed to be "off the ground" and that we could certainly use her able assistance, if she was still interested. She wrote back to say that she had talked it over with her family and decided she would come to New York.

From the outset, she was a trusted right hand. She took over the office management and many details of the work that were to keep the Christophers a smooth-running enterprise in the busy years ahead.

In the beginning, each person in the office (and there were about four) had to be a "jack of all trades." But as work expanded through the years, departments were formed and each had a specific job. In every instance, the work has been blessed with devoted and zealous workers.

But before I get ahead of myself, let's go back to the Christophers' early years. When our small office force was organized, the next step was to schedule the regular publication of *Christopher News Notes*—a four-page bulletin that would be sent free of charge to anyone requesting it.

Its purpose was to present practical suggestions, showing how persons in any walk of life could do something by prayer, word and deed to apply divine principles to modern life. Examples of what individuals had done along this line would be included.

After one experimental issue that seemed to hit the mark, we started distribution on a regular basis. At first, copies were limited not only by the very modest funds available but also by the fact that they were mailed to only about three or four thousand people. But by the end of the first year the *News Notes* had a circulation of about forty-five thousand, a number that doubled in the next twelve months. Today they are sent to more than a million persons throughout the United States and around the world. The same policy is still maintained—no charge and only by request.

From the beginning, each person who cared to play a part in the Christopher movement has had to do so entirely on his own. Suggestions and examples were given via the *News Notes* and through the talks I was frequently asked to give, but the application of principles was left entirely to each individual. This, I felt, would foster apostolic resourcefulness and initiative in those who accepted the idea. After more than a decade and a half of experience, I'm convinced it is a sound approach.

Launching the Christopher movement was like dropping a pebble into a pool. The circles just went on widening outward by themselves. Aside from the *News Notes* and the talks, I didn't do much more to further the idea for the first year, since I was still involved in directing Maryknoll promotion work.

As more individuals became aware of the Christophers, however, visitors began coming to our little office. Some wanted to ask questions, while others came to talk about the idea and make sure they had grasped its meaning. Many, too, either came or wrote to tell of their experiences in trying out the idea. Much of the information and many of the ideas that found their way into future *News Notes* and later into books came from this constantly growing reservoir of interest and experience.

In the autumn of 1946, just after the start of the movement, I had a most unusual visitor. He was an ex-Communist who had worked in Moscow for years, training workers to infiltrate the United States and weaken our country from within.

The Communist high command, he told me, was aware of the drift away from religion and moral principles in America. They were sending their emissaries to hasten this destructive process in every way they could, chiefly by getting jobs on newspapers, in movie-making, book publishing and magazines—all the major channels of communication where they could subtly slip their ideas into the thinking of the American public.

If they could help foster the feeling that religion was "old-fashioned" and high moral standards "impractical," they knew what would follow: an increasing indifference and disrespect for any authority, growing confusion about vital issues, and a gradual breakdown in family life. Then the time would be ripe to penetrate the government itself.

He told me that he had finally broken with Communism when he realized that the "brave new world" held up as bait to its followers was not the real goal; that the real goal of Communism was enslavement of the world's peoples rather than alleviation of their sufferings.

He managed to escape from Moscow and get to the United States. He had promised himself that if he was successful in reaching this country, he would try to make up for any harm he had caused by participating in the conspiracy against us. He had already told his story to the authorities and was now trying to alert everyone he could to the dangers of Communism.

He had come to me, he said, because he was alarmed and frightened that so many people he talked with refused to believe that such a diabolical plot could make any headway in this country.

In his estimation, this disbelief and almost apathetic attitude could well be our undoing. Our only hope, as he saw it, was to get as many individuals as possible to take a positive approach, along the lines the Christopher movement was trying to promote.

Then he came up with a most interesting remark. He said: "The Christophers could never have been started, nor would the idea make much of an impact without a missionary vision and drive behind it." He made the point that we would turn the tables on the Communists only if we started thinking and acting with as much vision and daring as they have.

We talked a little longer in this vein and then my visitor got up to leave, but not before giving this parting shot: "You're going to have to work fast and on a big scale if you hope to get as many people to work as hard for good as others are working for evil." I have never forgotten that warning.

At the time this ex-Communist came to see me, the Christopher movement was new, small and little-known. But even then it was apparent that the idea on which it was based was powerful in ways that are still unfolding.

By 1948, our mailing list was still constantly growing and each issue of the *News Notes* was going to every corner of the United States, as well as to many other countries. Although the *News Notes* were effective and I certainly intended to continue with them, I knew that after the bulletins had been read, they could easily be lost, misplaced or thrown away. So I went to work on a book that incorporated the ideas expressed in the *Notes*.

I soon found that the preparation of a manuscript, even by this method, is no easy job. But I kept at it, with the valued assistance of Charles Oxton, a sympathetic and competent writer. In November 1948, the book was published by Longmans, Green and Co. with the title *You Can Change the World*.

To my joy and relief, it was well received. *The Saturday Review of Literature* went so far as to say that it contained "a simple, explosive, contagious idea. And if ideas are as important as we have been taught to believe, this one may in truth 'change the world.'"

CHAPTER XI

WHAT ONE PERSON CAN DO

While I was still working on *You Can Change the World*, I drove up to Maryknoll one weekend in May and stopped off en route to see my friends, the McKeons, in Chappaqua, New York. I was delighted to find that Daniel and Louise McKeon had picked the same day to drive down from their farm in Ridgefield, Connecticut, to visit Dan's mother. We had many things to talk about, but since the new book was very much on my mind, I naturally told them about it and its theme—what one person can do, with God's help, to change the world for the better.

Dan was quick to express interest but Louise was a little hesitant. Her interests, naturally enough, were centered on their six children and their home, not to mention the sixty-four cows and the other responsibilities that made their farm a busy place.

"I'm afraid this idea of yours is for other people, not for me," she said amiably. "After all, I have my own little world —my husband, six children and the farm. Besides, I'm buried in the middle of Connecticut."

I was strongly tempted to let the subject drop. But I thought it might prove worthwhile to add one thought.

"Louise," I said half-jokingly, "even if you were buried in the middle of Alaska, it's still your world and you have as much responsibility for it as anybody else."

That was all the discussion there was about it, and conversation turned to other things. I had no notion of it then but my one little comment had an effect far beyond anything I expected.

After returning from Mass on Sunday morning, August 8, 1948, Louise picked up the news section of the New York *Times* and found herself horrified by a story on the front page.

"Dan," she cried, "listen to this!"

The article that caught her attention told of the kidnaping the day before of Madame Oksana Kasenkina, a middle-aged Russian woman who had been brought to New York from Moscow to teach the children of the Soviet delegation to the United Nations. Ten days earlier Madame Kasenkina had been told that she was to be sent back to Moscow. Her passage had been arranged aboard the Soviet ship *Pobeda*. While her superiors thought she was packing to leave, the teacher disappeared. It was not until after the ship sailed that the Soviet delegation learned she had managed to reach Nyack, New York, about twenty miles up the Hudson. She had gone to ask protection at the home of Countess Alexandra Tolstoy, the elderly anti-Communist daughter of the famous Russian novelist Leo Tolstoy.

Countess Tolstoy had readily agreed to do what she could to help Madame Kasenkina stay in the United States and apply for American citizenship. But both women failed to reckon with the determination of the Soviet authorities, who concocted a plan to remove Madame Kasenkina from Countess Tolstoy's home. It was so utterly unexpected—so "impossible"—that the abduction was successful, and Madame Kasenkina was driven posthaste to the white stone mansion on Sixty-first Street in New York City, which then housed the staff of the Soviet Consulate.

Up to this point, the abduction has few characteristics that were unusual. The Russians had seized the schoolteacher in Countess Tolstoy's presence, forced her into their car, and driven her away. But with her arrival at Consulate headquarters, the situation became unique, even bizarre. Unlike most kidnapers, Soviet Consul Jacob M. Lomakin not only told reporters that she was in the building, but actually invited them in and introduced Madame Kasenkina to them. Then he assured them in her presence that she had left Countess Tolstoy's home willingly and that she wanted to return to Russia. He even added that having been "rescued," she was now "under his protection." Despite appearances that plainly testified to the contrary, the frightened woman agreed to all that he said.

This was the story that Louise McKeon read to her husband on Sunday morning, August 8, 1948. At that very moment, hundreds of thousands of other newspaper readers were reading the same story and were probably equally as shocked by the almost unbelievable details as Louise McKeon was. But there seems to be no record of any other person who reacted as Louise did.

It was clear from the way the story was written that the *Times* reporter was unconvinced of Madame Kasenkina's desire to return to Russia. The look in her eyes and the nervous movements of her hands belied her words. Even if the account had made no reference to these telltale signs, Louise McKeon instinctively felt that Lomakin's story was untrue. She said as much to her husband, and he agreed.

"But what can be done about it?" Louise demanded.

Dan pointed out that, since the house in which the Russian teacher was being detained was Consular property, it was beyond the reach of the New York police or even of the Federal Bureau of Investigation.

"But there must be something that can be done," his wife insisted. "Can't we do something?"

Here was sure evidence that this busy mother had developed a new point of view in the six months since I had seen her at Chappaqua. At that time she had been entirely serious in telling me that the Christopher idea was not for her—that she had her own little world, and that she was "buried in the middle of Connecticut."

She was still in exactly the same place, but obviously she was no longer "buried." Half an hour earlier she had never heard of Madame Kasenkina. Even now she didn't know whether she could pronounce the name correctly. But the story of the friendless woman being forcibly held in the Soviet Consulate had deeply touched her.

"Dan," she insisted, "we must do something about it."

Her husband argued in vain that no one but the State Department could deal with the problem. But Louise wouldn't give up, and when her brother, Peter Hoguet, who had recently passed his bar examinations, came up from New York later in the day, they talked to him about it.

Peter was equally stumped.

"Well, the woman's been kidnaped," Louise insisted, "and we can't allow a thing like that to happen in our country."

"Listen, Louise," he finally objected, "forget it. After all, it's none of our business."

It was at this point that the woman who, six months before, had been living in her "own little world" made a penetrating remark.

"What do you mean, 'it's none of our business'?" she countered. "If it's not our business, whose is it?"

Neither her husband nor her brother had an answer to that. But the next day, back in New York, Peter still couldn't shake off his sister's questions. He finally talked the matter over with an experienced lawyer and decided he would try to do something.

According to the newspapers, Madame Kasenkina was still being held in the Soviet Consulate. Peter began to wonder if it might not be possible to obtain her release by means of a writ of habeas corpus. It seemed to him that this was about the only procedure which might work. Two days after his return from Connecticut, he had the necessary papers prepared and presented them to Justice Samuel Dickstein of the New York Supreme Court.

It was Peter Hoguet's contention that the woman in whose interest he was acting was being held in the Soviet Consulate illegally and against her wishes. His presentation was so convincing that when he left Judge Dickstein's chambers he carried with him a writ of habeas corpus which ordered Jacob Lomakin, the Soviet Consul General, to appear in court at ten o'clock the following morning—Thursday, August 12, 1948—and to see that Oksana Kasenkina appeared with him.

This was real progress, but a very serious hurdle lay ahead. Before the writ could take effect, it had to be "served" on the Consul General personally and placed directly in his hand. It couldn't simply be mailed to him or given to an aide to deliver. This would not be easy, since the Soviet Consul General was a difficult person to reach.

According to legal custom a lawyer does not serve his own summons, so Peter Hoguet asked another young lawyer to help him. The two met at the Hotel Pierre, across the street from the Consulate. Neither of the young men knew what to do next. It would be easy to ring the Consular doorbell, of course, but they had to place the writ in Lomakin's hands, and unless they could, nothing would be accomplished.

The young men considered their problem from every possible angle, but could come up with no foolproof plan. Suddenly they saw a big black car drive up and stop before a cluster of reporters at the entrance to the Consulate. Lomakin himself stepped out!

He had only to push his way through the knot of insistent reporters to enter the building and place himself out of reach. Peter knew he had to act instantly. The writ was still in his own pocket and there was no time to give it to his friend. Despite legal custom, he would have to serve it himself. Without pausing to explain, he dashed through the door of the Pierre and ran across the street, hoping against hope he would not be too late.

The reporters did their best to stop Lomakin and question him, but he thrust them aside and strode to the door. Fortunately, it was locked, and while he searched for the keys, Peter Hoguet dashed up with the writ in his hand. Realizing that the Russian would never willingly accept the writ, the young lawyer quickly leaned forward and thrust the document down inside the Consul General's coat.

Angered by this action, Lomakin pulled the paper out to throw it away. As he did so, Peter Hoguet knew that he had achieved his goal: the writ was actually in Lomakin's hand and, by all the rules, the summons had been served.

When court opened the next morning neither the Consul General nor the kidnaped woman was there, and widespread complications were beginning to develop.

In Washington, the Soviet Ambassador, Alexander Pan-yushkin, had issued a statement insisting that the story about Madame Kasenkina's being held against her will in the Soviet Consulate was not only "inadmissible" but was also "incompatible" with Soviet dignity. The State Department, acting on the complaint from the Soviet Embassy, sent an urgent message to Governor Dewey to ask whether Justice Dickstein could be prevailed upon to postpone things until Lomakin could take the matter up with his superiors, and the State Department could establish Madame Kasenkina's diplomatic status.

The judge felt compelled to order Peter Hoguet's writ of habeas corpus held in abeyance. Without the young lawyer's knowledge—or anyone else's outside the Soviet Consulate—plans were being laid to smuggle Oksana Kasenkina aboard another Soviet ship sailing late that very night.

New York City can be a very lonely place at any time. But on August 12, 1948, it is doubtful that any of its millions of people felt half as friendless and alone as the middle-aged Russian schoolteacher who was locked in a third-floor room at the back of the Sixty-first Street Consulate. Because it was a hot day, the single window was open. Now and then, the troubled woman looked out. All that she could see, in addition to a glimpse of the street and the walls of nearby buildings, was a narrow, paved courtyard below her window ledge.

In talking with her later, she told me that when she was so generously welcomed in Nyack by Countess Tolstoy, she thought her problem was solved—a problem she had lived with for more than eleven years.

In 1937, in the middle of the night, she and her husband, also a teacher, had heard a loud banging on the door of their little Moscow apartment. They had opened it to the secret police, who seized her husband and took him away. No word ever reached her of the charge brought against him, and she never saw him again.

With that experience behind her, she had hoped ever since for an opportunity to escape. She had kept this dream of freedom to herself, of course, and had done the best she could to give an impression of utter subservience to Communism. The masquerade was so successful that she had been chosen to teach the children of the Soviet delegates in New York. Here she thought she would surely make an escape. When her attempt had failed, there was nothing to look forward to but death or imprisonment after her return to Russia.

As she paced about that room on August 12, she was scarcely conscious of the little radio playing in her room. She had been given an injection the day before, which had befuddled her mind and weakened her will. Its effects had not entirely worn off. If her captors had known that she understood a little English, the radio probably would have been taken away. But there it was, playing softly. It made no impression on her until the music stopped and an excited voice began to talk. Suddenly, she heard her own name.

A moment before, she was sure that no one in the world cared what happened to her. But now, shocked into attention, she heard the radio announcer talking about her. Her command of English was limited, but within a minute or two, she had caught enough to understand that she was not alone, that someone, somewhere, was interested in her problem.

She listened and then hurried to the window. To her astonishment, as she looked past the corner of the house, she saw that an excited crowd had gathered before the Consulate. Their presence, she felt certain, was connected with the radio report.

The voice was still talking. She couldn't be sure what it was saying, but she got the impression that some legal action had been taken in her behalf.

And suddenly she thought she knew why the crowd had gathered. Her captors had obviously refused to comply with whatever order had been issued and the crowd was here to protest. But she knew better than they that their demonstration couldn't help her. In another few hours she would be outside the territorial limits of the United States and on her way back to the Soviet Union. As she stared out the window she saw a number of policemen keeping the crowd in order. If only she could get to them, she would be safe!

Even as she went to the door and tried to open it, she knew in advance that it would be locked. There was no way to leave the room except by the window. She could see that, though there was a concrete-paved court three stories below, a telephone wire angled across it only about ten feet below her window. It was too far to reach, but if she jumped to it, it might break her fall.

She climbed onto the window sill and leaped.

The telephone wire did break her fall and saved her life, although her hand was nearly severed by it. Hours later, she awoke to find herself in a hospital room—bandaged, bruised and sore. But she knew she was beyond the domination of the Consul General and was free at last, protected by the laws of a free people.

The Kasenkina case aroused public opinion both here and abroad against Communist tyranny. Consul General Lomakin and a number of other Soviet officials were recalled to Moscow. I followed the events as they happened, along with millions of others. And, like other Americans, I rejoiced in Oksana Kasenkina's courageous escape, an escape that few knew had been triggered by Louise McKeon.

It took many weeks for Madame Kasenkina to recover from her injuries, but long before she did, she had a request to make. She asked to see Louise McKeon, the person who had initiated this dramatic series of events.

About a month after Madame Kasenkina's leap for freedom, DeWitt Wallace, publisher of *The Reader's Digest*, invited me to lunch with the magazine's editors. The *Digest* had scheduled a condensation of *You Can Change the World* to appear the following April. Now they wanted to discuss the possibility of doing more articles on the Christophers. When I told them the story of Louise McKeon and her brother, Peter Hoguet, and the role they had played in the

Kasenkina affair, Mr. Wallace immediately assigned the late Fulton Oursler to do the piece.

The article, entitled "Whose Business Was It?" appeared in May 1949. It was also included in all the foreign editions of *The Reader's Digest*. Through it, millions of readers here and abroad learned how far-reaching one person's power for good can be—one person who, in this instance, had been bound up in her own little world six months before—one person who needed only a passing comment to make her realize "It's my world, too."

This case opened great new vistas for me. In exemplifying "what one person can do," it certainly indicated the relatively minor role "an outsider" like myself played. In this instance, it was nothing more than a little word of challenge that, in God's mysterious plan, turned out to be a decisive factor in getting Louise McKeon to set in motion a chain reaction that had worldwide implications.

It is always a never ending source of delight and surprise to see the unique ways that individuals choose in trying to make their influence for good felt. Once they realize that they are not working alone—that the Lord actually works in, with, and through them—they show unusual resourcefulness and perseverance.

The Kasenkina case was a striking reminder that the Christopher idea had tremendous potential, and it gave new impetus to my efforts to encourage the hopeful proposition, "You can change the world."

CHAPTER XII

CHALLENGE ON ALL SIDES

Christopher work grew so fast that it soon became apparent
that I could not devote the needed time and attention to it,
as well as continue to direct Maryknoll work in New York
City.

Bishop Lane, who had so generously encouraged me all
along, decided to appoint Father Joseph English to supervise
Maryknoll operations in New York and thus leave me free to
tackle the many and varied challenges the Christopher idea
was presenting. I still lived at the Thirty-ninth Street house
and was gratified to know that Bishop Lane expected me to
keep a hand in Maryknoll activities.

The Christopher staff had expanded to about fifteen
people by then, and it looked as though it would probably
continue to increase. We were obviously outgrowing the
limited space Maryknoll could loan us, so I began to think of
where we might establish our future office.

Before making any move, however, it was necessary to obtain the permission of His Eminence, Cardinal Spellman,
Archbishop of New York. He was most gracious in granting
this and so the search began. After extensive "looking" in
the midtown area, I finally found suitable quarters at a
reasonable rental, on the fourteenth floor of the Great Lakes
Carbon Building at 18 East Forty-eighth Street—coinciden-
tally enough, right next door to the small building in which

I had opened the Maryknoll office just eighteen years before.

On October 1, 1948, we moved into our new headquarters. Almost immediately new and fascinating challenges began to open on all sides. These were sparked to a large extent by the publication of *You Can Change the World* and its condensation in *The Reader's Digest*, as well as by the Madame Kasenkina story.

The book and the two articles reached an enormous audience, and the attention of millions was drawn to the work of the Christophers. We received literally thousands of new requests for information. By this time four hundred thousand people in the United States and overseas were on the regular Christopher mailing list. As I wrote at the time, "God willing, this tiny spark may one day burst into flame."

With the Christopher movement out of the incubator stage, I began trying to think of more ways to develop this sense of "personal mission." The *News Notes* and the book *You Can Change the World* had brought heartening results. But I knew that the most effective exterior action had to come from a strong interior spirituality.

For one reason or another, however, most people don't devote much time to developing this quality. They tend to get entangled in the cares and burdens of daily existence and forget the big meaning of life. If some sort of pattern could be devised that would encourage individuals to set aside even a few minutes a day to pray and meditate on such questions as: "Why am I here? Where did I come from? Where am I going?" it could help give countless individuals a perspective of eternity.

Individuals dominated by this outlook will want to do more than just get through each day; they will want to make it count for something. This was the spiritual note, the motivation, that I wanted to inject into the lives of everyone I could reach through the Christopher movement. Without it, I felt that the candle that had been lit might flicker out.

To have this objective was one thing, but to translate it into a practical formula that would appeal to the general public was another matter. For a long time I had been trying one experiment after another and was satisfied with none of them.

One day a friend dropped in.

"What are you working on now?" he asked.

I explained that I was trying to come up with a pattern for a brief daily meditation that would help the average person live a more purposeful life.

"Are you still fooling around with that idea?" my visitor asked, obviously unimpressed. "You've been at it for years without getting anywhere. Why do you keep wasting your time on it?"

I didn't know how to reply. Was I hanging on to an idea that really wasn't workable? I couldn't help but remember some other occasions when I had been equally determined with less good reason. Both the long bike ride over the mountain when I was a youngster and the tennis court at Maryknoll when I was a seminarian had taught me that some "impossible" things can be done if you are willing to work at them. So why not this? I knew there was a tremendous potential for good in the "thought-a-day" idea, so I pushed on.

I decided to call the series I had in mind "Three Minutes a Day" in the hope that many people would be willing to set aside at least that small segment of time for reading, reflection and prayer.

I felt that the format should stress both human and divine values and should also stimulate the reader to be an active participant rather than a passive onlooker in shaping the modern world. I finally arrived at four basic ingredients: a human interest story would start the meditation, followed by a supernatural application that could be obviously drawn from the story, then an appropriate passage from the Holy Bible and, lastly, a short simple prayer. Altogether, the four ingredients shouldn't run more than one page in a book.

This seemed to be it, but before I went too far I decided to try a few out on some people who could evaluate the appeal —or lack of it—objectively. Their reactions were so encouraging that I prepared about fifty of the stories.

Having progressed that far, I took them to Ralph Beebe, one of the editors of Doubleday & Company. After thumbing through a few he said his firm would publish the book if I would complete the manuscript with a selection for each day of the year.

While I was working on this book, its potential value was pointed out in an unusual way. One spring day in 1949 a man telephoned and asked to see me. His name was Whittaker Chambers. All I knew about him then was what I had read in the newspapers—that he was a one-time Communist, and that he had accused Alger Hiss, a former State Department official, of giving secret information to the Kremlin. Though I had no inkling of why he wanted to see me, I told him to come around. He arrived on a Saturday morning. The office was closed, but I was busy working on the *Three Minutes a Day* manuscript.

It was obvious from the moment he walked in that he was deeply disturbed. He was a rotund man, smooth-shaven, and of medium height. His face bore signs of worry and tension.

I offered him a seat and asked what I could do. He told me, very simply and sincerely, that he needed spiritual help.

I racked my soul in search of some specific suggestions that might give him the strength and courage he was seeking, but I couldn't seem to come up with the right thing. Then I had an idea. Reaching into the pile of typewritten pages that lay on my desk, I pulled out a single sheet. It was the selection for Good Friday from the *Three Minutes a Day* book.

Handing it to Mr. Chambers, I said: "I don't know whether this might help or not."

He took it and, without saying a word, proceeded to read it.

This is a day of failure (the typewritten copy began) but failure only from a human point of view. It is the failure of the years of life that precede the triumph which will last for eternity. For every true Christopher, Good Friday should be a pointed reminder that being a Christbearer also means being a crossbearer. Christ Himself could not have put it more specifically: "If any man will come after Me, let him deny himself and take up his cross daily and follow Me." (Luke 9:23)

Christ doesn't force us one inch. He leaves things entirely in our own hands. But if we—of our own free will—decide to carry Christ into the marketplace, we must not merely be ready for endless trials and tribulations. It is our business to go out and meet them. Again, as Christ pointed out: "He that taketh not up his cross and followeth Me, is not worthy of Me." (Matthew 10:38)

With each of us the failure of the cross must go before the final triumph. We must be willing to fail and fail again—even to be crucified—in order to play our part in saving the world.

That was all that the page contained, except for this final simple prayer:

Teach me, O Jesus Crucified, to take up my cross each day cheerfully and without hesitation.

I watched Mr. Chambers as he read, and his expression seemed to change. When he rose to his feet, he continued to glance at the sheet of paper before leaning forward a little and thoughtfully putting it on my desk.

"That's just what I came in for," he said quietly.

Then he took my hand, pressed it, softly said "Thank you," and left.

I never saw Whittaker Chambers again but I followed with deep interest the reports of his self-assurance when he confronted Alger Hiss, and the steadfastness with which he played out his role.

This incident sent me back to my work on the *Three Minutes a Day* manuscript with renewed confidence and vigor.

Fortunately, the simple formula imposed few restrictions on the selection of material. One, for example, was based on the story of the photographer whose advertisement read:

As you look to me	$1.00
As you think you look	$1.50
As you would like to look	$2.00

To the story I added this brief comment: "There is the everlasting temptation to pretend to be something we are not. Many headaches can be avoided by following the simple advice: 'Be yourself!' If God gives us only one talent, He wants us to use it efficiently; but He certainly does not wish us to try to fool the public—to give the impression that we have five or ten talents."

Another story originated in a visit I had made to the Tower of London many years before. On the stone wall a prisoner, some three centuries before, had carved: "It is not adversity that kills, but the impatience with which we bear adversity."

Using this incident, I wrote: "Rebelling against difficulties or obstacles that cannot legitimately be avoided only makes a bad situation worse. Ordinary common sense recommends that we ride the storm, not buck it. But going one step further —going from the natural to the supernatural—makes it easier to bear adversity patiently."

It was not too difficult to add a missionary significance to these human interest items. One concerned a high school girl who was seated next to a famous astronomer at a gathering and, knowing nothing of his background, was not sure how to open the conversation.

"What do you do?" she presently asked.

"I study astronomy," he replied.

"Really?" said the teen-ager, wide-eyed. "I finished astronomy last year."

My point for this story was made in the following comment:

"Many people stop growing mentally and spiritually at an early age. Physically, they continue to develop, but spiritually they remain as six-year-olds. Yet most of us—like the famous English writer and teacher who had the habit of listing his occupation always as 'student'—do recognize that we have a lot to learn, especially in those things which concern us spiritually."

I hoped that some of the suggestions would help people rise above the obstacles that keep so many from being Christlike workers. For instance, I included this story about the Devil putting on a display of his most effective tools:

"Pride, Jealousy and Malice, of course, were recognized by most people, but there was one worn, tiny, wedge-shaped tool that bore the highest price.

" 'What is it?' someone asked, 'I can't quite place it.'

" 'Oh, that!' Satan answered, 'that is Discouragement. It is my most valuable tool. With it I can open many hearts, since so few people know that it belongs to me.' "

The book *Three Minutes a Day—Christopher Thoughts for Daily Living* came out in the fall of 1949. Over 150,000 copies were sold before it was published in a paperback edition, a form it has remained in ever since, selling another half-million copies.

Doubleday sent a copy to a newspaper syndicate with the suggestion that a daily column might be made up from the stories in the book. Before I fully realized just what was happening, fifty newspapers were using the material, and more were showing interest.

Encouraging as this was, it presented a new problem. I had prepared only 365 stories for the book—just enough for one year. But if a newspaper column attracted readership interest, it could go on indefinitely. And that is just what happened. Long before the newspapers published all the first 365 stories, it became clear that I would have to keep writing more if the column was to continue.

A second series of Three-Minutes-a-Day stories began to take shape. When they added up to 365, a new book called *One Moment, Please* was released. Year after year the demand has continued, and book after book has appeared under such titles as *Just for Today, Make Each Day Count, It's Your Day,* and the like.

In time it became apparent that the first title—*Three Minutes a Day*—was the one that stuck in the minds of our readers. So in 1959, after seven other titles had been used, we decided to go back to the original. We called the one for that year *Three Minutes a Day (Volume 2)*. Since then, Volumes 3, 4, 5 and 6 have appeared, and more are in the works.

The idea that had taken so long to get off the ground continued to expand. Now, well over a million copies of the books are in circulation, and 103 daily newspapers across the country regularly feature the newspaper column based on these Christopher stories.

A new idea for their use popped up in 1954. Through it, people have been reached who might not have been touched at all by the books or the newspaper columns. As ideas go, there was nothing earth-shaking or highly original about this one. It was simply to use these meditations for short "spot announcements" on the many radio stations that span the country.

Since the appeal of the Three-Minutes-a-Day concept had been demonstrated, I decided to offer the stories, free, to any radio station interested in them. I knew that one-minute announcements were the usual thing, so I trimmed the format down in order that each item and comment could be read in fifty-five seconds.

I prepared a number of samples and sent them out to various radio stations with a letter promising to provide the necessary recordings free in return for one minute of air time for a program to be known as "Your Christopher Thought for Today." The proposal was most generously received and, at this writing, 1,900 radio stations—nearly half the total number in the country—are using these selections every day.

Early in August 1958 I received this letter from the program director of a broadcasting company in Florida:

As Program Director of this radio station, and also as master of ceremonies of our morning show, may I take this opportunity to thank you and the Christophers for sending us the "Thought for the Day" transcriptions which it has been our pleasure to use for the past five months.

I use these on my morning show, one each morning, followed by a hymn, as a "Thought for the Day and Hymn for the Morning" feature. I've had more comment about your little messages than anything else on the whole three-hour program, and of course all the comment is favorable. One morning I mistakenly played the same message I had played the day before and, believe me, I heard about it via mail and telephone. "What have you done to Father Keller?" they asked. I had to play two the next day to make up for it.

One of your messages last month dealt with the advantages of letting people know when they had done something outstanding, instead of merely complaining. Hence this letter, sir. You are doing an outstanding work for people of all faiths. I happen to be Jewish, but I look forward to our "daily thought" each morning as much as my listeners, and I wanted you to know that we do really appreciate them, and take them very much to heart.

Letters such as this have reassured me that people everywhere hunger for spiritual nourishment as much as they do for their daily bread. It is a deep consolation to know that we have been able to supply even a tiny crumb of that nourishment.

CHAPTER XIII

INTO MOVIES AND TELEVISION

One of the problems—though a pleasant and challenging one —that grew side by side with the Christopher movement was the constantly increasing number of requests for talks.

It had proved to be such an effective way of reaching people that, in the spring of 1949, I decided to go on a cross-country tour, speaking in as many places as I could. While I was in Los Angeles, at the western arc of my swing, I had a free afternoon, so I accepted a less taxing invitation. Robert McMahon, a young lawyer with Warner Brothers Studio, had suggested a game of golf at the Bel Air Club in West Los Angeles.

It was a beautiful day and the course was in wonderful condition. My game was typical of one who seldom gets on the golf links, but my host didn't seem to mind playing with a duffer. He was also a very good listener, so naturally I was off on my favorite subject—the Christophers.

On the ninth tee, I hooked my drive well into the rough, just as I was telling him how much I regretted being able to accept only one out of every twenty invitations to speak on the Christopher idea. There was no time for discussion while we hunted for my ball, but as soon as we were back on the fairway, Bob McMahon went right on with the conversation.

"You'll never be able to catch up with the requests for talks if you just keep on the way you're going."

Since I thought I was doing the best I could, I must have looked a little puzzled. But not after Bob's next remark—

"You couldn't catch up," he continued, "if you gave five talks a day. Why don't you put the idea into a movie? That way you could give five hundred talks a day."

He didn't have to say another word. Once again, the Lord had sent a valuable suggestion in an unexpected way.

I didn't know a great many Hollywood people by any means, but through the years my work had taken me in and out of Los Angeles and I had met a fair number. My introductions had begun several years before when a group of producers, directors and actors who had heard of *You Can Change the World* asked me to talk to them about it. At the end of that particular meeting, one producer told me that he felt the Christopher approach made good sense. "I've been here in Hollywood for fifteen years," he said, "and I've made lots of movies in that time, but I can't remember ever putting any-one connected with government or teaching in a particularly flattering light—now I'm going to see what I can do to change that."

Leo McCarey, of *Going My Way* and *The Bells of St. Mary's* fame, was also there, and he came up afterwards and said: "Be sure and let me know if there is anything I can do for you—I would be glad to help."

Irene Dunne and her husband, Dr. Francis Griffin, were at that first meeting, too, and afterwards Irene asked if I would come and give a talk at their house. I said I would be glad to, but added that the only time I had open was Christmas Day. Before I could say anything more, Irene came right in with: "What difference does it make? Christmas is as good a day as any." And as it turned out, it was.

About fifteen were on hand when I arrived. As with the first group, they were predominantly in the creative end of film work—producers, directors and writers.

The next time I was back in Los Angeles—about five or six months later—the Griffins invited another group for a "Christopher evening." This included Rosalind Russell and Fred Brisson, the Gary Coopers, and Loretta Young and Tom Lewis. Through them, in turn, I grew to know others. They were always most friendly and receptive to what the Christopher idea was trying to promote. When it came time to pursue Bob McMahon's suggestion about making a Christopher film, it seemed providential that I had met such generous and talented people.

My first call was to Leo McCarey. Fortunately he was free, and within the hour he waved me into a chair and I was telling him as enthusiastically as I could about Bob McMahon's idea. Leo was sympathetic, but being "an old pro," he saw difficulties that I had missed entirely.

"Have you got any miracles up your sleeve, Father?" he asked. "If you have, you'd better use them. You need a script. You need a cast. You need a lot of money. And even with all those it's almost impossible to make an interesting picture out of a speech."

He shook his head.

"Just the same," he mused, "I like the Christopher idea. Let's give it a try."

During the next few weeks, back in New York, I did my best to get together material for the picture in the hope that it would turn out to be more than a pipe dream. I sent it on to Leo McCarey. A few months later I got word that a tentative script had been worked out. Leo suggested that I return to Hollywood to help put it in final shape, assemble the cast, and film the picture.

When I arrived in November, the first thing we decided on was the name. Leo suggested that we capitalize on the recognized title of the book, *You Can Change the World*. That taken care of, we turned to the cast. Lining it up could have been the cause of untold problems, but the angels were with us and it began to take shape with almost unbelievable ease.

I mentioned it first to Irene Dunne and Loretta Young, and they offered to participate right away.

The next thing we knew, Jack Benny suggested that we use a set representing a gathering of stars at his home. As word got around, the ball kept rolling.

"It's the first time I ever saw anything like this happen," Eddie ("Rochester") Anderson remarked. "I was going to Mexico for a vacation, but I wouldn't miss this."

Ann Blyth, William Holden, and Paul Douglas also volunteered their services and, almost before I fully realized how astonishing all this was, two writers were hard at work on a new script.

I began to understand what Leo McCarey meant when he said: "It is almost impossible to make an interesting picture out of a speech." Although the film had to present the facts I used in my talks on the Christophers, some way had to be worked out to put action and variety into presenting them. Eventually, though, the "almost impossible" was hammered into a workable reality. The film was to be set in Jack Benny's "house" and he was to invite the various actors and actresses of the cast to come so I could explain the Christopher idea to them. They would lighten the whole thing with comments, questions and appropriate interruptions.

Even though the general format was arranged, new developments kept evolving. In one scene I was to point out the four explicit references to God in the Declaration of Independence. To add color to the explanation, Johnny Burke and Jimmy Van Heusen whipped up a special song and called it "Early American." The script was altered to make room for the piece and Dennis Day volunteered to sing it. Things looked a little bleak when Dennis came down with a bad cold the day before the scene was to be shot. But even this liability was turned into an asset when Leo McCarey mentioned Dennis' misfortune at a party attended by Bing Crosby.

"How about me?" asked Bing. He was working on another picture, but he showed up bright and early the next morning to go through the song a couple of times and learn his lines. Before the morning was half over, the whole scene was shot and Bing was on his way again.

With Bing Crosby a part of the cast, it was only natural for Jack Benny to remark that it was too bad Bob Hope was out of town. That sparked an entirely new idea. The script was revised to include a scene showing me on the receiving end of a telegram.

"It's from Bob Hope," ran my new lines. "He wants me to phone him."

"Oh, I'll get him for you," Jack Benny was to say. "He lives here in Hollywood."

"Maybe so, Boss," Rochester chimed in, "but the telegram says he's in Houston, Texas."

When Bob returned to Hollywood, a scene was filmed showing him talking on the telephone, supposedly from Texas, with a ten-gallon hat on his head. In the inimitable Bob Hope manner, he expressed his wide-eyed astonishment that Jack Benny was actually footing the bill for that long-distance call.

All the members of the cast except myself were competent, experienced actors and actresses who played their parts with remarkable effectiveness and ease. But whenever the camera turned its searching eye in my direction, I broke out in a cold sweat. It was a workout I'll never forget. In one scene I was struggling through the story about Madame Kasenkina and Louise McKeon. The other members of the cast were supposed to be hanging on my words. Leo McCarey knew perfectly well that I was no actor, so he had arranged to take my part separately. I was grateful for his consideration but, even so, I knew my words were not getting over. Finally, Leo stopped the cameras.

"Listen," he told me. "I thought you wanted this story of yours to reach millions of people. But it won't impress ten people the way you're doing it now! I know this is a new experience for you. And I know you're tired. But you've got to tell this story as if you really mean it. Now let's try it again."

I knew he was right, and this was just the jolt I needed. I had been telling myself that I simply didn't know how to go about "playing" a part. But after Leo's remark I began to realize that if I really wanted to stir up a personal sense of mission in the countless thousands of people who might see this movie, I had better begin to communicate it with every fiber of my being.

So I went at it again, trying to forget my inadequacies and concentrating on the importance of what I had to say. Thanks to Leo McCarey's insistence on trying to share my story with countless others, rather than merely reciting facts, the results were far more effective.

Every single member of the cast had performed in the movie without charging a penny. Hal Roach, whose studio was used for shooting the picture, was clearly impressed.

"You've got a million-dollar cast!" he exclaimed. And it was true.

The director, the script writers and the song writers also generously donated their time. Bernard Carr, the independent producer who took care of all the studio arrangements—the sets, the background details, and the props—kept our costs so low that when the picture was released our total expenditure was only about $25,000—a real "bargain" by movie-making standards. I didn't know, at first, just how all the money would be raised, but by the time the film was completed it had come in and mostly in small contributions ranging from one to five dollars.

Fortunately, prints—or copies—could be bought for as little as $30 apiece, which was the actual cost to us. Still, it was with a deep breath at the start of 1950 that I ordered 100 prints. But before long I was able to let my breath out again as 500 prints were made and distributed. In the ten years or so during which the picture has been shown, roughly 3,000 prints have been bought by churches, clubs, individuals, schools and organizations of every kind.

The record for showings by one person is probably held by a woman in Florida who used her print 110 times. A man in Indiana showed his copy 50 times. Those who bought the picture paid for it out of their own pockets and made all the arrangements for showing it to what must have been a total audience of hundreds of thousands and possibly millions of people.

Robert McMahon's idea that one Christopher movie would be equal to "five hundred talks a day" certainly struck the nail on the head.

Through the years, the casual setting of a golf course has provided many another interesting and worthwhile meeting. It certainly never had anything to do with my abilities at the game, however. Lacking the time to practice or play much, I never progressed beyond the duffer stage. Occasionally, however, friends asked me to join them and I was always glad of the opportunity for exercise and the mutual exchange of ideas.

After *You Can Change the World* was completed, Jack Benny invited me to play six holes with him early one morning. Jack wasn't in the pro ranks, but I was worse. He used to get very annoyed when he missed a shot, and couldn't understand why I didn't get upset.

One day he asked: "What do you do to keep calm, Father?"

"I just say a prayer for the souls in Purgatory, Jack."

To which he countered: "Well, maybe that's what we all should be doing. We might play a better game of golf, though there's no guarantee from your score."

On another occasion, I remember having hit an unusually long, straight drive, which is always a pleasant shock to one who doesn't play too well or often.

Jack was just as surprised as I was and said: "How did you ever pull that one off?"

"Oh, I just trust to the Lord," was my prescription.

All Jack could say about that was: "That's the trouble, people like you always have the Lord helping you."

It always interested me to see that Jack went about the sport with the same meticulous attention to detail that has kept him in the forefront of stardom for so many years—a quality that could be transferred with advantage to any field of endeavor.

Another interesting early morning golf game with Christopher implications was a round I had with the writer-director team of Bill Perlberg and George Seaton. I often wondered if conversation about the Christophers was boring to friends, particularly when they were out to have a relaxing time. But invariably, once the topic was brought up, the conversation kept moving in that direction.

I remember on that particular day, we were going up the fourth fairway at Hillcrest when Bill said that if the Christopher idea was developed on a large enough scale, it could change the whole of Hollywood. Then he told me about an idea he and George had for a film which, as it turned out, was *Miracle on 34th Street*. They asked me what I thought about it, and all I said was that it sounded as if it had the makings of a great picture and I hoped and prayed it would come to be. With a few further words of encouragement, the conversation turned to other things.

About a year later, George Seaton wrote to thank me for my boost and to say that their "little dream" had come true. When the picture was released, it proved to be a success from nearly every standpoint. Of course, all the credit certainly goes to George and Bill for pursuing their plan and sticking with it until they achieved their desired result. But in its own way, this incident typifies the favorable manner in which the Christopher approach has been received by those who are anxious and willing to maintain high standards in all areas of entertainment.

From the beginning, one of the major Christopher points has been to promote positive and constructive ideas in this area. When *You Can Change the World* created such widespread interest, the natural progression seemed to be some dramatic presentation of the Christopher idea in regard to the communications field. So we got to work on ideas and a script, and the following year *Television Is What You Make It* was produced and directed in New York by Jules Bricken. Starring Ruth Hussey and Walter Abel, it was a half-hour dramatization of the responsibilities of a television producer, and the fact that valuable service can be rendered by those who take up television as a career.

A third picture, *Government Is Your Business*, was also slated for production in New York, but Jules Bricken moved to Los Angeles so the film was made there. Arthur Franz was featured as the courageous young man who demonstrated that good government is possible once enough citizens overcome their apathy and take an active part, on whatever level, in actually running it.

The widespread acceptance of these and later films made me wonder about the possibilities of television. I discussed the matter with several persons who were experts in this new medium. They agreed that stations would no doubt be interested, but they warned me that for a program to have any impact it would have to appear every single week. Presentations would have to be filmed well in advance of showing and, for all practical purposes, would have to have a drastically lower budget than our other films.

That knowledge was hard to swallow, but I was not ready to give up. I talked to the late Hugh Rogers of the New York advertising firm of Batten, Barton, Durstine and Osborn. I frankly admitted that the cost of making a weekly film might very well price us right out of the market, but asked him if he knew where I could find a producer who could turn out what we needed "fast and cheap."

"The man you want," he replied, "is Jack Denove."

Jack, I found, had left BBDO a short time before to start a production company of his own in Hollywood. I got in touch with him the next time I was on the West Coast and we outlined a series of fifteen-minute programs.

There was a lot of work to do before we could actually begin, so I went back to New York to gather material for the first twenty films. The arrangement was that Jack Denove would produce and direct, and I would line up the content and arrange for the guests who were to appear in the various presentations.

During the 12 years that the Christopher program has been telecast, the many stars I have asked to participate have been wonderfully generous with their time. Many have come over and over again and always most willingly and graciously. I remember being in the midst of a filming in California, shortly after Joe E. Brown lost his house and many valuable paintings, plus a lifetime collection of irreplaceable personal possessions, in a tremendous fire. I certainly hesitated to bother him, but when he heard that we were filming, he called to say that he would be delighted to be of service.

Robert Young was another "regular" in Christopher films. He came once to read a series of points we had prepared on the worthwhile use of time by those who had reached retirement age. After he went through the prepared script, he started to ad lib. According to Bob, he was one of the group these points were aimed at. He had more or less retired from a full schedule at that point and had looked forward to a life of leisure. But after a few weeks, he said that he had called all his friends, played innumerable games of golf, and didn't really find this "take it easy" pace very satisfying. "We have to have something to live for—we can't just sit around looking for ways to amuse ourselves and keep busy." The way he shared his views with the audience certainly gave much more validity to the points we had asked him to present.

The very individuality of those who have appeared in "star" capacity in Christopher films through the years has added a great plus to Christopher programs. It has been a privilege for me to work with these men and women, and they have been responsible in no small way for the wide acceptance of the idea through the various film series.

But to get back to the beginning. The first series of films was produced very cheaply and in remarkably short order. When it came time to get them on the air, I went to see Hugh Rogers again. He suggested that I personally visit as many television program managers as possible. This would mean a lot of travel, of course, and it would take a lot of time, but if it got the films on, I felt it would be well worth it. Before starting my tour, I wrote to the various program managers, outlining the idea of the Christopher series and offering the films without charge, in return for free air time.

The letters went out early in 1952 to the hundred or so television stations then in operation. Sixty-eight stations accepted the offer immediately, so I never found it necessary to go on the road.

Up to this writing, about 500 filmed programs have been made for the Christopher series, which appears weekly on some 300 television stations, or nearly one half of the operating outlets in the United States and Canada, plus the Armed Forces networks. Even if each program attracted an average of only 10,000 viewers per station, it would be seen by at least 3,000,000 people a week.

Ideas and themes for Christopher programs and publications seem to pop out of almost nowhere. One day, in a casual conversation, I heard someone remark that George Washington "was not a spiritual person." I don't know why, but I felt affronted by this statement and decided to do a little checking for myself. Before long I found so much information that proved the contrary that I started to prepare a script for use on television.

During the period of research, I went on a lecture trip that took me well into the South. I mentioned what I was doing to some friends and, as good fortune would have it, they knew a lady in Atlanta, Georgia, who had an unusual collection of material about George Washington. My friends felt sure that she would be glad to let me see it. As a result of a long-distance telephone introduction, the generous collector offered to send me some of her books and papers by air express.

They contained so much fresh and pertinent material that it was possible to make six half-hour films on the spiritual side of Washington under the over-all title *George Washington Speaks for Himself.*

With the generous aid of twenty-one actors and personalities, they were shown on the hundreds of television stations that carried the Christopher series throughout the country.

The presentations were: *Washington as a Young Man*, with Ward Bond, Joe E. Brown and Ruth Hussey; *Washington as Commander-in-Chief During the Revolutionary War*, with Barbara Britton, Mrs. Bob Hope, Art Linkletter and Pat O'Brien; *Washington's Inner Life During the Revolutionary War*, with Ray Bolger, Jerry Colonna and Harry Von Zell; *Washington's Efforts for the Constitution*, with George Fenneman, Adolph Menjou and Jane Wyatt; *Washington as Our First President*, with Eddie Cantor, MacDonald Carey and Don Wilson; and *Selections from the Life of George Washington*, with Fred Allen, John Daly, Ella Raines and Thelma Ritter.

All the films were based on authenticated letters and speeches, and revealed Washington's great spiritual strength in many different ways. For example, at a time when the Revolution was going none too well, and the outcome was anything but clear, he wrote a friend:

"We have . . . abundant reason to thank Providence for its many favorable interpositions in our behalf. It has at times been my only dependence, for all other resources seemed to have failed us."

His strong spiritual quality was just as evident in happier times. On December 23, 1783, when the war had been won and he went to Annapolis to resign his commission, he commended "the interests of our dearest country to the protection of Almighty God, and those who have the superintendence of them to His holy keeping."

Six years later, when he took the oath of office as President of the United States, he not only swore to preserve, protect and defend the Constitution to the best of his ability, but also ended his solemn oath with the words, "So help me God." This invocation is still used in official oaths by those taking public office, in courts of justice and in other legal proceedings.

The deeply reverent attitude of our first President was far more than personal. On September 19, 1796, in his memorable Farewell Address, he once again gave public testimony to the importance of religion and morality in the conduct of good government when he said: "Of all the dispositions and habits which lead to political prosperity, religion and morality are indispensable supports."

Other great men of American history have also been featured from time to time in the Christopher series. In showing how these patriots integrated positive and constructive ideals, both human and spiritual, into public and private life, we hope to encourage today's listeners to emulate their example.

Along with historical presentations, the Christopher series has included interviews with homemakers, teen-agers and teachers, as well as with persons in government, labor, business, science, the newspaper field, magazine and book publishing, radio, television, motion pictures, art and advertising.

The programs are addressed to persons in every walk of life, and in each instance guests have emphasized in a relaxed, informal but practical manner how one person can make a distinct contribution, with God's help, towards changing the world for the better.

They have covered such topics as the need for excellence on the part of all citizens who wish to preserve and protect the blessings of freedom; the contributions that can be made in the medical field by those with a high sense of dedication and competence; the rewards gained through an understanding and appreciation of art; the contributions, hardships, and fulfillment of a career in the field of social work; the important and vital services rendered by people in all facets of government; the need for individual prudence and self-reliance in the many problems and aspects of economic life; the necessity of guiding young people to work towards a lifetime career in which they can do more than earn a living; the responsibility of audiences and of those in the creative end of the communications fields; the contributions average citizens can make towards the over-all needs and improvement of schools; the influence the home can exert in raising the standards of the marketplace; and the part that individuals and nations can play in meeting the needs of the underdeveloped and underprivileged countries of the world.

The value of good reading has been highlighted in several of the current film series. We have been fortunate in having Mrs. Eleanor Smith of the Brooklyn (N.Y.) Public Library present a "look at a book" segment, which appears on a Christopher program about once a month. With understanding and humor, Mrs. Smith has discussed well-known classics as well as modern fiction and nonfiction. Each book has been chosen for its potential appeal to a general audience and as a means of stimulating a wider interest in worthwhile reading.

Through the years we have evolved a format which we follow for most of our Christopher television programs. They usually open with a brief human interest story from which I draw a spiritual application suggesting how every person can do something by prayer, word and deed to blend divine values into every phase of human affairs.

Immediately following this introduction, I interview the guest for six or seven minutes. During this visit I become a listener, so that the guest may use as much of the short period as possible to explain his work or experience and offer basic proposals of action suitable for the general audience.

When the interview ends, I give a three-minute talk emphasizing the spiritual motivation that each person should have if he wishes to be a truly effective force for good in today's challenging world. I cite examples and give suggestions which I hope may prove both helpful and stimulating to any person who wants to "light a candle" rather than "curse the darkness."

In conclusion, I read a few verses from the Holy Bible, and end with a two-minute sermonette based on the Scriptural passage. In it, I try to remind listeners that God has given each of them a mission in life to fulfill, a mission that is assigned to no one else, and that every person without exception can do something to restore the love and truth of Christ to the marketplace.

The informality and relaxed manner in which the programs are filmed has surprised most guests who appear in them.

The concept of making a movie or television program has awesome overtones for most people who are not directly involved in the field. Scripts, rehearsals, makeup and run-throughs are all terms that seem to be part of any normal production. So it's quite understandable that the Christopher setup is somewhat of a shock.

We always try to get the best results with the least possible expense. This calls for speed and efficiency. The former sometimes proves a bit disconcerting for participants at first, but they are usually pleasantly surprised with the end product.

I remember making one series several years ago at the Fox Movietone Studio in New York when William Nichols, the editor of *This Week* magazine, was appearing as a guest. He had arrived while we were in the middle of a "take" and was directed to the makeup room. By the time he came back, we were ready to film again, so he was ushered right into the set, which, incidentally, is designed to look like the Christopher office. Although we had had a telephone discussion on the points we would cover in the film, Mr. Nichols assumed there would be some sort of rehearsal on the spot. But time means money in filming, and we try not to have any breaks between the films except for mechanical adjustments. We usually hope to complete eight fifteen-minute presentations a day. Most producers count on three to ten minutes of final footage, so ours is considered somewhat of a phenomenon, and would never be possible without the speed and efficiency of Jack Denove and the generous cooperation of an expert crew.

As is the case in each of the films, the director came up to give Mr. Nichols a few points about which camera to look into and how to handle the notes he had with him, and the head cameraman checked the lighting before the cameras started to roll. Mr. Nichols looked a little surprised and turned to ask what he should do then. With the thought of reassuring him, I said: "Don't worry, Bill, just leave it to the angels," and with that we were on.

As with each guest who has appeared in our films, Mr. Nichols gave a fine presentation. There is a certain spontaneity when there has been no rehearsal, and those who are in a position to speak with authority on their subject come across with a naturalness that would not otherwise be achieved. Afterwards, Mr. Nichols agreed that the angels had done their job nobly.

The close scheduling unfortunately doesn't leave much time for visiting with guests before or after the "take," but everyone has been very understanding of this once the reason is known. In most cases they are delighted that the filming hasn't taken up more than an hour or so of their busy day.

Guests come in and out with such frequency that attendants in the studio sometimes aren't quite sure who's who. I remember one year a teen-age boy appeared on the set, all made up and seemingly ready for a film. I saw him and was frantically trying to think who he could possibly be. But the mystery was solved when the director asked his name and what he was going to discuss. Our unknown "guest" said that it was all a big mistake—he was a messenger on his way to another set and, when he had come in, some helpful soul had assumed he belonged to the Christophers and rushed him into makeup.

This was an unusual bit of comic relief but it was also an example of the cooperation of everyone that has ever been involved in Christopher film work. Whoever sent the messenger to makeup knew we had a heavy schedule and a slim budget and assumed this would expedite things.

Once people realize the constructive, hopeful idea behind the Christophers, they want to pitch in and do their part to make the work successful. This is true all along the line, from the producer and director to the cameramen, sound men, electricians, grips, and makeup experts. We have been fortunate in having many of the same people back year after year. I often think they must be bored with the same format and listening to me over and over again. But the efficient way they do their jobs and the attention they give each guest is another instance of the way individuals in every walk of life enter into the spirit of the project without the slightest prodding from anyone. It becomes their project.

A sampling of one day's mail shows that this thought carries over into the audiences who watch the completed programs on television.

From Newport, Rhode Island, and Little Rock, Arkansas, came two requests for material we had presented for young people. One asked for *Tips for Teen-agers*, with the comment: "It is a wonderful program—long may it live." The other inquired about *Points on Writing*. The sender said: "I work with teen-agers and can use these helpful suggestions."

Since the same program is not shown the same week on each station that carries the Christopher series, one day's mail covers a variety of topics. For instance, on a single day a card from Hawaii asked for the material on parliamentary law, and one from Lincoln, Nebraska, brought this remark: "Your program on labor and management was one of the best I ever heard in my long life in that field." Another from Toronto, Canada, included this observation: "The stories about Lincoln and Washington were inspiring. There are things which a person gets out of this type of program and never forgets."

Comments like this are reassuring, of course, but they also serve as a very graphic reminder of what needs to be done in the future—more, for instance, that would encourage those like the man from LaCrosse, Wisconsin, who wrote: "Your TV hour has been the one reason for my remaining in a difficult public service job."

Reactions such as these are heartening evidence that, through the many individuals who so generously give of their time and talents to our telecasts, the Christopher idea is reminding countless persons week in and week out that each and every one of them is delegated by Almighty God to play an important role on the stage of life—and that an eternal reward awaits those who, despite hardships, leave the world better than they found it.

CHAPTER XIV

PEOPLE ARE WONDERFUL

Much is said and written about the apathetic and self-centered attitude of individuals today. While there may be some truth in this complaint, it has been my happy experience to have had personal contact with thousands of people who are going far beyond self-interest in working for the good of others. There are no doubt millions more like them—in low position and high—who would do the same if motivated to release the hidden greatness that God has entrusted to each of them.

In human affairs, practically everything that has ever been accomplished for good or evil throughout the history of the world began with one individual. Whether in the field of the arts, sciences, government, education or homemaking, scores of men and women, as individuals, have been at the heart of events and directions.

One unique example of this is Philip Cancelleri, a barber in Southampton, New York. I met him in September 1947, after a talk I had been asked to give there. At that time, there was great concern in the free world about how the Italian national elections would go the following April. Since many of his relatives were in Italy, Mr. Cancelleri was particularly disturbed about the possibility of a Communist victory at the polls. After my talk that afternoon, he came up to introduce himself and tell me about a plan that he thought might do some good.

Before outlining what he had in mind, he told me that since he had come to the United States in 1913, he had married, raised a family, and generally found life to be good. For this reason, he said that he was greatly bothered by the flood of criticism about what was wrong with free government and the world in general. And what irritated him most was that those who did the greatest amount of complaining never did much to improve conditions.

He then went on to say that he wanted to get individuals of Italian descent to start a letter-writing campaign to their relatives and friends in Italy, warning them of the importance of voting for freedom at the polls the following April. He asked me what I thought of the idea. As in the instance of Louise McKeon, my only part in "operation letter-writing" was a word of assurance and encouragement.

During the next few months, Mr. Cancelleri kept me posted on his efforts "to light a candle." He started on a small scale by writing to his own relatives and those of his wife, telling them about life in free America. Then he got his oldest son, a doctor, and his oldest daughter, a nurse, to write to some of their friends.

He knew that these limited personal contacts could hardly make a substantial difference in the outlook of an entire country. So he contacted various newspapers and organizations to ask their cooperation. Invariably the idea met with a warm reaction but also with regrets. The project was too big for them to handle.

But Philip Cancelleri wouldn't quit. He continued to ask his friends who had relatives in the old country to lend a hand. Gradually—providentially—the idea caught fire. Businessmen, young G.I. brides, housewives, veterans groups, civic societies and religious leaders joined the cause. What started as a steady trickle of letters soon became a torrent. Literally millions of letters went out from people in every section of this nation to their relatives and friends in Italy. This vast number of people, each acting individually, accomplished what no agency or official group could possibly have done— they reached the hearts of the Italian people.

The Russian foreign office complained that a major factor in the Communist defeat in that Italian election was the letter-writing from overseas. Little did the Reds realize that it had all been started by one man—a barber in Southampton, New York.

Several years later, when the Christophers got into television, I felt that stories such as Philip Cancelleri's could and should be told as an example of what one person can do. If the person involved could do the telling personally, so much the better. So when we planned our first filming in New York in the fall of 1952, I asked Philip if he would come to the city and appear on one of our programs. His reaction was an immediate "yes." He was quick to see that it was an opportunity to tell others that if one person like himself could set off a chain reaction of such far-reaching magnitude, so could they.

Although television was obviously a new experience for him, Philip spoke with an authority that came from conviction and experience. The interview was a very moving one and drew reactions from thousands of listeners.

Every case is not as dramatic as this, nor does it have such widespread consequences. But each in its own way emphasizes the validity of the Christopher theme, "You can change the world." When individuals find what can be done by following this idea, they usually want to encourage others to look for their own ways and means of acting in a positive and constructive way, too. Those who have been guests in Christopher films have demonstrated this over and over again.

A particularly enthusiastic example of this is Dr. Edward

Luboja, a dentist whose office is in Radio City, New York, just two blocks from Christopher headquarters. He told me that for some time he had led a pleasant and uncomplicated existence with family and friends in a suburb of New York City. Then one of his friends gave him the Christopher book *Government Is Your Business*.

"My conscience was bothered," Dr. Luboja said, "and I decided I'd better get busy and take a little interest in local politics."

He went on to say that it was most discouraging at first. The meetings seemed almost calculated to bore any newcomer, and those with vested interests were not anxious to explain what was going on. But having gotten his feet wet, Dr. Luboja wasn't about to give up easily. He went to meeting after meeting, asked questions, and requested explanations of issues at stake. He went one step further and prevailed upon his friends to come with him and bring their friends, too. As a result, attendance at meetings more than doubled in a year.

What was most appalling to Dr. Luboja was the discovery that in his town many people in politics seemed to have an ulterior motive, and only a few were concerned with the over-all interests of the average citizen. This struck home. He felt that if more individuals realized this point, they would make it their business to find out, among other things, where their tax money was going.

When I asked Dr. Luboja if he would like to present his views on one of our television shows, he said he would really welcome the opportunity to tell some of his experiences and point out how and why an average citizen with high standards can become active in politics for the sake of good government rather than personal gain. His willingness to participate typifies the response of most people when they realize that through the Christopher program they may be able to give a wide coverage to the basic ideas and principles they themselves are promoting.

The importance of blending the spiritual and human in every facet of life was highlighted in a unique way by Anita Colby, the recognized beauty and fashion expert.

She has been a wonderful friend of Christopher work for many years, and in her own particular field has done an outstanding job of reminding millions of women that the exterior picture they present is a reflection of the inner self.

Anita has appeared on several Christopher programs through the years, and I remember on one she told the audience that when she was in Hollywood working with new stars, she geared her work to help them bring out their particular individuality and personality. I asked her if she would capsule some of her advice for our listeners. In doing so, she stressed that each one has a special talent that must be enhanced and developed in the fullest possible way.

"First of all, recognize your own capabilities," Anita said. "Then set yourself a high and handsome goal, but not a wildly unreachable one. Once you've decided on your destination, never think of the word 'impossible,' and make progress every day.

"Whatever you're doing now, do it superlatively; it will only make a greater person out of you. Just one thing—in the process of 'getting there,' don't forget the rights and feelings of others. If you think about other people—really try to help others—it will show in your face." That, in essence, is the beauty expert's formula.

All the tips Anita incorporates in her talks, books, and news columns are aimed at reminding women of all ages and backgrounds that they have a particular contribution to make —and that their ideals should be brought from the home to the world. In doing so, Anita said that their true femininity is the most beautiful cloak they can wear.

It has been a privilege for me through the years to meet with the many guests who have appeared in Christopher films. The audience response has always indicated that they, too, have derived much inspiration as well as practical suggestions from these individuals.

One of the best-known and -loved figures in public service is former President Herbert Hoover. I did not know Mr. Hoover personally, but a good friend of the Christophers, Mr. Neil MacNeil of the New York *Times*, had worked for many years as his editorial assistant and mentioned to me that "The Chief" would probably be willing to appear in one of our television programs. So we invited him, and to everyone's delight he accepted. Even among the small group at the studio, there was no mistaking the profound respect and admiration his visit evoked.

In the filmed interview, Mr. Hoover stressed the importance of encouraging young people to take up government service as a career. "I have always believed that no able-bodied citizen can refuse to serve his country in a crisis," Mr. Hoover said. But then he added that much more than crises had to be considered, for vast numbers of accomplished and skilled employees are needed to conduct government on a day-to-day basis. This includes, Mr. Hoover continued, not only the elected officials—all the way from the precinct worker to the President—but also the millions in civil service. Quite obviously, citizens should be interested in who these people are and in what kind of job they are and will be doing, Mr. Hoover pointed out.

In discussing the work of the two Hoover Commissions, the ex-President said that the reorganization of civil service had been a special aim. One reason for this was to make government attractive to American youth—youth with character, an attribute of paramount consideration.

Pursuing this point, I remember saying to Mr. Hoover dur-

ing the filming that he himself had always been admired for
this particular quality and had been an inspiration to millions
because of his devotion to a cause and his giving of self.

When I asked him about his unusual ability to get others
to work for him, he answered with the typical sincerity and
humility that have won him the respect of so many throughout the world. He said that most good citizens are willing to
serve their country and, since you want only good ones, you
only have to ask. "Call and explain the problem and you will
find, in most instances, that they will come," he said. As an
example, he cited those who worked on the two Hoover Commissions. Out of 350 persons—mostly volunteers—that he
invited to assist him, he had only three refusals, and these
for very good reasons—such as one man who had broken his
leg just an hour before the call came.

Giving the audience the opportunity to hear from such
outstanding personalities as Mr. Herbert Hoover has always
been a great privilege for me. Each is an example of constructive "doing" in his own right and has made an important
contribution in pointing out practical ways that can help
members of the audience make the most of their own opportunities to serve others.

Quite a different field was touched on in another program
by Dr. Edward Teller, the world-famous nuclear physicist,
who now teaches at the University of California. He pointed
out how atomic energy can and is serving mankind in a constructive way. For some time, I had admired the statements
Dr. Teller made about his work, but did not feel that I understood the many aspects of his field sufficiently enough to
discuss them with him on television. Some friends of mine
who knew him, however, felt that he might be willing to appear in one of our films and present his convictions on the
peaceful uses of atomic energy. They suggested that we all
meet for dinner and discuss the possibilities. He happened

to be visiting New York at the time of one of our filmings, and dinner was arranged. I went with some trepidation, but it was a delightful meeting and Dr. Teller graciously agreed to come the next morning to appear as a guest in one of the programs.

The points he made were both hopeful and realistic. He emphasized the positive values that could be achieved if the atom were harnessed as a servant of humanity. He gave two examples. One concerned a rich mineral area in the United States, between the Rocky and Sierra Nevada Mountains. Through atomic explosions these deposits could be brought closer to the surface for more efficient mining, Dr. Teller said. The second example given was on the other side of the world and involved water supplies in Australia. As Dr. Teller explained it, the land on the ocean side of the mountains along the coast is fertile and tillable, but that on the other side is arid. Blasting through this block could open vast new areas for cultivation and development.

In discussing the over-all concept of atomic energy, Dr. Teller emphasized how important it was for the average individual to understand that this great power can be controlled and guided into the right place and used for the right purpose.

Persons with big vision usually have a desire to share it with others. Another such individual is General Carlos Romulo. He has been a good friend of mine over a long period of time and has appeared in several Christopher films. Starting out as a cub reporter and copyeditor, he became the Philippine representative to the United Nations and helped write the Charter. Later he became president of the General Assembly, and in his most recent post in this country he served as the Philippine ambassador in Washington. I was happy to introduce him on one program as "a man with the courage of his convictions."

During our conversation that time, he stressed the important role that each one can play in promoting peace. He pointed out that prayer, for instance, was within everyone's grasp, and went on to advocate friendship for all people as most important in this world effort. General Romulo defined a foreigner as "a friend I have yet to meet."

In concluding his remarks, he cautioned that the future of the world could well depend on whether or not freedom would triumph over Communism in Asia. He cited the 1955 Bandung Conference as an example of how twenty-nine Asian nations could work together in spiritual rapport. The Conference, General Romulo emphasized, showed the great good will and respect people have for freedom.

Another friend who has been a guest several times on Christopher programs is Mr. Robert E. Murphy. He came first while he was Under Secretary of State, and made a "return engagement" after he retired from government service. In each film visit, Mr. Murphy, too, stressed the great contribution that can be made by individuals who choose a career in government. In telling of his own involvement in the field, he explained that it started more or less accidentally, since a leg injury had prevented him from entering the army. Over the years, however, he was often involved with the military. One much publicized event was the key mission during which he accompanied General Mark Clark into North Africa before the invasion.

Mr. Murphy told us that only 25 per cent of foreign service posts are political appointments. His own career spanned several administrations, and his assignments took him to many trouble spots around the world. Mr. Murphy's inspiring service gives his words of advice an authority and conviction that cannot help but influence listeners to raise their sights to the vital issues of our day.

Through the years of Christopher filming, many guests

have touched on the subject of youth and the need for leadership training at this level.

Eugene Kinkead of *The New Yorker* magazine and author of the Christopher Award book *In Every War but One* made this point in an unusual and rather frightening way. He had served as a correspondent with the Pacific Fleet in World War II and had found that in the Korean War, ten years later, there was a distinct change in the character and stability of many servicemen. The Army was studying the problem, and Mr. Kinkead was given permission to research for a book on the topic. Both were hunting for the reason why so many American servicemen had made such a poor showing under Communist prison-camp interrogation.

In his book, as well as on the Christopher program, Mr. Kinkead described the weakening of family life as the basic cause. Schools and churches, he said, can give a great deal of fundamental training, but the family is the first source of strength and the strongest bond. The gradual breakdown of this cradle of society in the relatively few years between World War II and the Korean conflict upheld his theory in a graphic and frightening way. His recommendation that spiritual as well as mental and physical training stem from the home is basic in the Christopher approach.

Another outstanding author who appeared in a Christopher film was Pulitzer prizewinner Mr. Bruce Catton. He has been called the foremost authority on the American Civil War. When I asked him how he got started, he said that his entry into the field was almost by chance. It came about when he found some Civil War narratives in an old bookstore in Washington, D.C. The natural curiosity of the newspaper reporter, which he was at the time, plus exhaustive research, eventually led to the writing and publication of the first volume of his famous trilogy on the Army of the Potomac. During subsequent years many other volumes followed, and in

1954 he launched the first issue of *American Heritage*, the magazine of American history. Mr. Catton's remarks on the importance of knowing our American heritage and the great value that is to be gained from a knowledge of the past were most provocative. As with each guest, they were more meaningful because they came from a recognized and respected expert.

The fact that each and every individual can make a constructive contribution to themselves and their families, as well as to their country and society as a whole, was brought out in a very inspiring way by Dr. Howard Rusk. As director of the Institute for Physical Medicine and Rehabilitation of New York University, he is considered a leading pioneer in this field. Largely through his efforts, the attitude towards disability has undergone a tremendous change. There are, Dr. Rusk said, some twenty-five million disabled people in the United States. Until a few years ago, they couldn't expect to live normal lives. Now 90 per cent can be taught some gainful work.

Regarding rehabilitation, Dr. Rusk continued, the world speaks a common language. As with any individual dedicated to a cause, he is anxious to tell as many people about it as possible. He has appeared on the Christopher program three times, and the audience has shown keen interest in each presentation. Over and over, he has pointed out that the patients he works with have a spirit that no completely well person can know about. Dr. Rusk believes that such spirit, together with modern knowledge and technology, can open untold new horizons not only for them but for those who work with them, and for all who can enjoy the benefits of their specific contributions.

"Art is the gift of God, and must be used unto His glory. That in art is highest which aims at this." So said Michelangelo, and to discuss this point as it applies to each one of us, we have been fortunate in having Mr. John Walker, director of the National Gallery of Art in Washington, D.C., as a guest on several Christopher programs.

In each visit he has stressed the rewards that can be gained through an understanding of the beauties of art. In one program he built his thesis around a quotation of Hazlitt. The eighteenth-century man of letters regarded museums as the mind's true home, and "the contemplation of truth and beauty, the proper object for which we were created."

Mr. Walker demonstrated the truth of this quotation by showing the audience four reproductions of paintings he considered to be most popular in the National Gallery. His choice ranged from the fifteenth-century "Adoration of the Magi," with its brilliant radiance of colors by Fra Angelico and Filippo Lippi, to his own favorite, a seventeenth-century Vermeer. He said that after a long, hard day, he often went to look at this particular painting on his way home, and never left without feeling refreshed and with a new joy in life.

His third selection was an eighteenth-century English portrait by Romney, and the fourth, a Van Gogh. When I asked Mr. Walker how many people had visited the National Gallery, he said that in the first fifteen years, some twenty-four million. He admitted that he was not one to follow figures, but added that on one Sunday he had inquired and was told that thirteen thousand people had visited the museum on that day alone.

By the time Mr. Walker made his third appearance on a Christopher film, in 1963, the figures had multiplied considerably, since the National Gallery had been one of the two host museums to the Mona Lisa. Well over a million and a half people lined up for a two-minute view of the famous Italian masterpiece while it hung in Washington and at New York's Metropolitan Museum. The attention of these crowds is perhaps the outstanding proof of the need and desire people have for "the contemplation of truth and beauty" that Hazlitt spoke of. Their interest went far beyond curiosity, Mr. Walker said, and crossed all age lines. School children and even babies were brought to see what so many considered the peak of artistic achievement and "to pay homage to the great genius of the Renaissance." As he prepared to accompany the Da Vinci masterpiece back to the Louvre, Mr. Walker reminded us that art is indeed a universal bond between peoples of all cultures and ages.

I have always admired Mr. Walker as a dedicated and highly articulate gentleman. He once said that he didn't know why he was paid for his job because, as he put it, "I love it so." This attitude is projected in whatever he does, and his understanding and love of art has helped to enrich the lives of countless individuals.

Most Christopher films—and all of the ones I have just discussed—are made in a studio. There have been a few exceptions, such as the one made on the Thunderbird Golf Course at Palm Springs, California.

The idea for it came in 1954 when I met Ben Hogan in Texas while giving talks there. My point in asking him to be on a program was to have him tell about the wonderful comeback he had made after a nearly fatal automobile accident.

The following year when I was making films for the Christopher series in Los Angeles, Ben was a visiting "pro" at one of the Palm Springs courses. I suggested that it was the ideal time for him to tell his story on a Christopher program. He agreed and, knowing that he was a friend of Bing Crosby and Bob Hope, I invited them to join us. Since they all played golf, the Thunderbird course seemed to be a natural setting. The "natural" idea proved to have many kinks, however.

We had to arrange for a filming crew and all the equipment

to be brought from Los Angeles. (Palm Springs is more than a hundred miles away in the desert.) In the interest of keeping expenses low, all the filming had to be done in a day, and since the sun went down below the mountains at 3:30 P.M., the working hours had to be between 9:00 A.M. and mid-afternoon.

But, thanks again to our producer-director Jack Denove, all the obstacles were met and overcome. On that occasion, his fringe operations included hunting for the sound truck, which got lost in the desert en route. He finally tracked it down at 3:00 A.M., just six hours before we were to shoot.

Since the crew had to start setting up cameras and sound equipment well before we started filming, it left them without much sleep. But, as always, those who worked on the Christopher program gave every bit of cooperation we could hope for or need.

When we went out to the golf course for the filming, we found that the four of us—Bing Crosby, Ben Hogan, Bob Hope and myself—weren't alone on the "set." A sizable crowd had gathered to watch the proceedings.

What they saw was a very informal operation. When Bob Hope "signed up" he had asked about a script. I told him there wouldn't be one and he seemed both amused and surprised. "That's the way they made movies thirty years ago," he said. "An Indian would jump off the cliff and someone would put the words in his mouth on the way down."

Ben's story about his return to championship golf after being told he would never be able to walk, much less return to an active sport, was an inspiring one. It was an outstanding example of what one individual can do once he puts his mind to it and has the courage and perseverance to follow through in spite of seemingly insurmountable obstacles. After he told it "on camera," I asked him if he would demonstrate a few "shots." For any golfer, it was an experience to remember.

While the program was entirely ad-libbed from beginning to end, I had prepared a few spots that I felt should be injected if the presentation was to make an impact from a Christopher point of view. Thank God, the finished product seemed to be fairly well balanced, but during the filming I kept wondering whether I was doing too much or too little in adding a divine touch to the lesson on a golf course.

We had planned that the last ten minutes of the half-hour film would be wholly on the Christopher points, so the director decided to have the four of us sit and chat informally. While we were getting ready for this sequence, Bob asked what each one was supposed to do. Everyone had been a little flustered by the unorthodox way we had been filming the picture, so by way of reassuring him, I said, "Don't worry, Bob, I'll lead." With that, he turned around to Bing and Ben and said: "Get that—he says he'll lead!" Turning back to me, he said, "Okay, Father, just touch your ear when I'm supposed to speak."

That set the pace and we were off. I told them of some of the cases that had come in the mail, which showed what and how people were picking up the Christopher idea and applying it to their own circumstances. The comments and questions of Bing, Bob and Ben set off the incidents in a light but forceful way.

When we came down to the last two minutes, I asked Bob Hope to close by reading the Christopher prayer—the prayer of St. Francis of Assisi. The timing was just about perfect. As the director called out that most welcome word "cut," the sun was starting to disappear behind the mountains.

Though the format and location for *Faith, Hope and Hogan,* as the program was titled, were unique in our series, the aim remained the same—to remind each and every individual that by the grace of God he has the power and ability to make a distinct contribution to life.

Several months after the picture was released, Dolores and Bob Hope asked me to a reception at their home. After greeting them, I decided it might be better to keep my distance in the crowd. I was sure that Bob was probably upset about the amateurish way we had done the golf course film. But I needn't have worried. Along he came with the remarks: "Where are the cameras and lights? When are we starting to work?" Then he followed up by telling me: "Everywhere I go, I hear very little about my own pictures—all people talk about is that one I did with the Christophers on the golf course." That comment was a relief, and an assurance that the "angels" were taking good care of Christopher films.

CHAPTER XV

THE POWER OF BOOKS

Radio and television provide a unique means of stirring up individuals to get into the thick of things rather than sit on the side lines. But as I discovered from the reactions to the first Christopher book, *You Can Change the World*, this medium also has distinct advantages.

Anyone sitting down to read a book is obviously willing to give it considerable time and thought and, thus, the contents are more apt to make a lasting impression. Then, too, it is always there for reference and can be passed along and shared with others.

The "every-person-a-missioner" idea featured in *You Can Change the World* appealed to a great many people as a novel challenge. The reactions we received showed how readers pursued it in a wide variety of ways.

Take, for example, the airline pilot and his involvement some years ago with the Parent-Teacher Association and the school board in his community. If anyone had a right to be excused from participating, he certainly did, since his New York–Kansas City run kept him away from home much of the time. Nevertheless, he was sparked by the idea that God expected him to carry his share of the load. So he decided to attend one of the PTA meetings.

Afterwards, when he was telling me his story, he said that everything about that first meeting had been very boring.

"I was determined never to go back to another," he said. "But then I told myself that if the wrong kind of people get control of our schools, it will be the fault of those who think as I did then."

Next thing he knew he was involved in a local school association meeting which turned out to be "anything but boring." The discussion centered on an official New York State proposal to put "an act of reverence" for God back into the public school program—a proposal that left each community free to decide the question for itself.

When he asked the various candidates for the school board how they would vote, their replies were disturbing and revealing. One actually maintained that no one had the right to question him on the subject. Another said that in her opinion the question should be decided by referendum. And a third refused to be pinned down at all.

"After the meeting," the pilot explained, "my wife and a few friends were surrounded by a hostile group, a few of whom actually shouted insults about both religion and government."

The situation became a real challenge, and he went to work with a handful of friends who agreed that a recognition of God should be restored to the schoolrooms of their community. He and his supporters felt sure that only a very small minority really objected to the idea of "an act of reverence." But to bring this fact to the attention of the community required a lot of leg work and perseverance. Ultimately they sent out a carefully prepared questionnaire to all the voters in the school district. To their gratification, out of 1,379 questionnaires that were returned, only 127 were against the proposal.

The wishes of the overwhelming majority were brought to light primarily through the efforts of one man.

A similar situation came to my attention one evening when

a man came up and introduced himself to me at a civic meeting.

"I'm a Baptist," he told me, "and some time ago I read your book *You Can Change the World*. I didn't believe it then, but now I want to tell you, I do believe it because I've tried it. I belong to a labor union of sixteen thousand members, but no more than about five hundred ever came to the meetings, and the officers had it all their own way. And not only that—they weren't interested in either the workers or the management. They were just using the union for their own benefit, and the whole business looked hopeless.

"But then I thought I'd try the Christopher idea and attend meetings myself. It wasn't very long before I got a chance to say a thing or two. And then I got others to come to the meetings and they, in turn, got a lot more to attend. We began to make progress, and before a year was up we had about seven hundred members who hadn't been attending meetings before—all new blood—and we got everything reorganized and voted in a whole new group of officers.

"So you see, I know from experience that one person is important."

A lady in Hartford, Connecticut, commented that she had always felt that her home and four children were enough for her to cope with until she read about the Christopher idea. Then, "I joined two clubs—one in my church, the other the PTA. It was the first step out of my quiet shell of isolation. Recently I was elected president of the PTA. . . . I have also had two articles published, which I never would have written without your encouragement."

In November 1949 a letter came from Bishop James Edward Walsh. After completing his term as Superior General of Maryknoll, he had returned to China and subsequently was made head of the Catholic Central Bureau in Shanghai.

Not long before the Communists were to take over China, he sent a few comments on *You Can Change the World*.

"I liked your book immensely, and a friend of mine here, a very wealthy Jewish banker, is reading it now and seems to like it equally. He wants to pass the book among some friends, so I told him by all means to do so.

"What we both liked in it particularly was the spirit of charity that breathes in it, the consideration shown for all points of view, the care used to avoid offending sensibilities while stating the Catholic attitude with every frankness. . . ."

Comments such as these assured us that we were on the right track in making use of books to present the Christopher approach.

Many of the reactions to *You Can Change the World* pointed towards the need for a book that would show "how and why" a person could dedicate himself to a career with a purpose.

So back I went into research. Every spare hour was spent on the correspondence, filing and clipping that eventually jelled into *Careers that Change Your World*.

The book was a long time in the making, but even while I was working on it, letters continued to assure me that the subject was well worth pursuing. One young graduate wrote: "During almost twenty years of schooling, I don't recall one instance where anyone suggested to me alternatives for life-work and their various degrees of desirability. . . . Get your Christophers before they take any old job that comes along."

A man in Orlando, Florida, wrote: "I am an ex-accountant now teaching in a junior high school. The Christopher book *You Can Change the World* was a deciding factor in my change of career."

There was a growing public awareness of the need for getting more competent people in every occupation. I hoped to capitalize on this realization by showing in a limited way how individuals could find job openings in such vital fields as government, education, radio and television, labor relations and social service.

After Doubleday published *Careers* in 1950, the contents of the mailbag showed that individuals were anxious to contribute and, in many cases, needed only a little nudge to get going.

A mother of six, for instance, started a school paper to boost interest in the PTA. Her efforts paid off and the membership increased from 50 to 122.

Four college graduates decided to go into FBI work because they were convinced they could do more than earn a living in such an area.

Another young man took a job in a university library, without much idea of what he was getting into. He wrote: "After a few weeks, I was amazed at the opportunities confronting me when students asked me for advice and suggestions in the preparation of their assignments."

A young lady who went into the field of social work sent me a letter that typifies the attitude of so many selfless and willing individuals who will sacrifice time and money once they realize that they can make an important contribution for the good of others. In part her letter read: "During the time that I have worked with the state agency, twenty children have been placed in good adoptive homes and hundreds more in foster homes and institutions, where many have for the first time a good bed and three meals a day. I have from time to time, I must admit, been tempted to try a job where I would be able to earn more money and get some of the material things that all young girls like, but then, I look into the eyes of some of my little children and I realize I have more than money can buy."

By themselves, these instances are not earth-shaking, but they are certainly heartening indications of the power that is there and that could, if sufficiently multiplied, be decisive in changing the world.

Just before *Careers* went to press, I spent a weekend at Cape Cod with the husband-and-wife author team, Fulton and Grace Oursler. When I told them about the new book, I explained that it had a double purpose—to show potential readers how they might find "jobs with a purpose," and also to start them thinking about "What's wrong with the world and what can I do about it?"

I asked them to look over the chapter headings and make any suggestions they thought would improve them. As always, they were very interested and added a professional touch that was most helpful.

When we had finished our work on this, Mrs. Oursler turned to me and said: "Why don't you write a book on good government?"

Having just put the final touches on one book, I was taken somewhat aback by her question. I did admit that I would be very much interested in seeing such a book, but felt I was in no position to write it.

"It's hard to find a book anywhere," she pointed out, "that shows in a popular way what the nature and purposes of government are, and where the individual fits in. And," as her punch line, she added, "the subject is very much in keeping with your theme, 'What's wrong with the world, and what can I do about it?'"

Our conversation bestirred me to visit several bookshops and libraries when I got back to New York. I was astonished to see how little material was available on government from this angle.

While I was still mulling the whole proposal over, I accepted an invitation to speak at New Rochelle, New York. Because the subject was actively in my mind, I referred to it. I pointed out that government on any level is good or bad in proportion to the number and quality of the people who are sincerely interested in it. I added that failure on the part of good people to take a part in what concerns the common good of all can be a serious sin of omission.

After my talk a businessman approached me. He said that I had neglected to mention what he believed to be one of the greatest single obstacles to good government. This, he said, was the failure on the part of most wives and mothers to understand and take an intelligent interest in political affairs.

"Without ever intending it," he explained, "they are doing more harm to the country than a carload of Communists. They do everything in their power to keep their husbands and children away from anything and everything connected with politics. To them there is no such thing as good politics—and I can vouch for this first-hand. My wife is a fine, sensible woman, but she certainly has a blind spot on this subject. On more than one occasion when I've wanted to do something about some political situation, she has raised such a fuss that I have just given up.

"Back of it all," he continued, "is the average woman's dread that her husband or her son may be publicly criticized, ridiculed or kicked around. They don't realize that by keeping good people out of politics they are leaving the field wide open for the incompetent or even worse."

What he said sent me back to my reading and investigating with renewed purpose. Before long, I collected some important and revealing facts.

One survey, for example, showed that 82 per cent of American parents who were asked if they would approve of their children taking part in politics stated that they would disapprove.

Another poll revealed that five out of seven of those who had been interviewed believed that all politicians are dishonest.

As I continued my spade work, I found that in many ways the attitude of our people towards politics and politicians left much to be desired. A book entitled *The Legislative Way of Life,* by T. V. Smith, included the following discouraging statement: "Democracy is government by politicians for citizens who too often reward them with disdain. This disdain of politicians is a dangerous disease. It is particularly dangerous for a democracy."

All of this brought me back to Mrs. Oursler's suggestion that the Christophers put out a book on good government.

I knew I could not write for the experts. But if I could make it clear to the average citizen that he has a responsibility before God to promote and sustain good government, perhaps it would accomplish a little of what Mrs. Oursler had in mind.

It was a long time before I could even outline a table of contents. There were books, magazines and newspaper articles to read, as well as local, state and national government officials and employees to meet and talk with.

The Christopher office was as busy as ever, but fortunately Father Edward Flannery of Providence, Rhode Island, had joined the staff. This new and talented member was to be an invaluable assistant during the next several years, and when work on the new book began, he was particularly helpful in its preparation.

As *Government Is Your Business* got underway, many excellent sources of information were made available, especially in Washington.

My first meeting there was with two officials of the Department of Agriculture. Neither was well acquainted with the work of the Christophers, so I gave them a brief rundown on the purpose of the work and why I was tackling this book. I explained that we hoped it would encourage more people with a love of God and country to go into government service. I told them that the material would not be technical—that

I had no plan of setting myself up as an expert on any phase of government—and that I felt it was even more important to encourage good people to go *in* than it was to get bad people *out*.

One of the two gentlemen was a dignified gray-haired man with many years of public service behind him. He listened intently as I outlined my idea and then said:

"If this book you are writing is able to bring more God-fearing people with a purpose into government, a wonderful thing will have been accomplished."

"And if you can do anything," his associate added, "to make people already in government feel that they are doing something worthwhile, you'll be doing a great deal, too. It is sad but true that when you tell anybody outside that you work for the government, they usually laugh and make some crack like, 'Oh, so you're one of those guys who lives off the rest of us!' "

The elder of the two, who had served many years under different administrations, then quietly made what was to me a shocking statement.

"I come from a little town up in New England," he said, "and when I go home, as I do whenever I can, more often than not I am almost ashamed to say that I am in the government."

This man of demonstrated ability and great patriotism could quite obviously have occupied a position of importance in private enterprise. The government and country were fortunate in having his services. Yet he was ashamed to admit that he worked for it.

It was not until I had left his office that I began to appreciate all that he had implied. Who, I wondered, were the people who made this man attach a sense of shame to the highly worthwhile work he was doing?

I felt pretty sure they were people like you and me, people

who meant no harm but who had fallen into that easy habit of being cynical and critical about everything and everybody connected with government, including even such individuals as this dedicated public servant who was actually doing a hard job and doing it very well.

Since the tone in which this official had spoken suggested his discouragement, I could not help but wonder what would happen if he decided that he had had enough, and resigned. How could the people of the country measure such a loss? If that happened, the thoughtless Americans who made him feel ashamed would have done as much to weaken our government as if they had been Communists.

As I talked with officials in other departments, I was impressed by their ability and understanding. One man who had formerly been a newspaper reporter gave me a vivid picture of the various phases of government in terms of the people who make it work—from the President and members of the Cabinet, through Congress and right on down to the messengers.

In the offices of the Atomic Energy Commission I talked with a lawyer, a former Naval officer and a one-time businessman, each of whom had given up a good and lucrative position in order to fill a job that each one of them considered important to the welfare of the country. In this still new arm of government, thousands of others shared their convictions.

At the State Department, I asked to see one of the officers in charge of personnel. When I was finally ushered into an office, the man behind the desk seemed quite aloof. But when I explained that I was working on a book which I hoped would influence competent, patriotic, God-fearing people to enter government service, his attitude did a complete about-face.

"You don't know how glad I am to see you," he told me. "I've been in this job for ten years, and at no time have enough really first-class people applied for the available jobs. So, of course, we often have to take those who are not first class. We are always hoping to find more and better people for the positions we have to fill. As a matter of fact, at this moment the State Department has three different teams of recruiters in various parts of the country looking for typists and stenographers, and we're always on the lookout for able people to fill more important positions, too."

I particularly thought of this conversation three days later, when on June 25, 1950, the Republic of Korea was invaded by more than sixty thousand North Korean Communist troops, and the bitter Korean War began.

I wondered then, and during the long drawn-out struggle that followed, why so many of our finest young men who willingly and capably performed their duty when they were called to war, were seldom attracted to the many equally important civilian positions in the federal, state and local governments.

In 1951, *Government Is Your Business* was finally published by Doubleday. Addressing "Mr. American Citizen," the publishers pointed out that the book was intended for him: "Either you run your government or government runs you." And then the statement added this reminder: "You—whoever you are—can do something to strengthen the United States of America."

There were four books behind me—beginning with *Men of Maryknoll* in 1943—plus the annual edition of *Three Minutes a Day*. But still another was beginning to take shape.

As I went about the country giving talks on the Christophers I had been surprised at how few people were aware of the deep spiritual roots of America. So often audiences were amazed to learn, for instance, of the frequent reverential references to God that are to be found in the great American political documents. The Mayflower Compact, for example, was signed "solemnly and mutually in the presence of God." The Declaration of Independence refers not only to "the laws of nature and nature's God," but also to the "Creator," to "the Supreme Judge of the world," and to the reliance of the signers "on the protection of Divine Providence." Even our one-dollar bill bears a picture of the "Eye of God" and our coins all carry the phrase "In God We Trust."

In 1835 Alexis de Tocqueville, the French statesman and political writer, pointed out: "The Americans combine the notions of Christianity and liberty so intimately in their minds that it is impossible to make them conceive of the one without the other."

He was referring, of course, to conditions as they were more than a century ago. Since then, many people have lost sight of the fact that, although the Constitution clearly prevents the establishment of any officially recognized state religion, there is nothing whatever either in the Constitution itself or in the minds of most Americans that stands in opposition to the idea propounded by the Declaration of Independence that ours is a nation under God. The whole concept of the Constitution implies this fundamental truth. Most Americans accept the fact that this nation was so founded. But, little by little, recognition of Him has come to be more and more ignored in our public schools. On many occasions, the opposition of an unbelieving minority has been imposed on the children of people who do believe in God.

In 1952, as I was thinking seriously about this subject, Protestants, Jews and Catholics alike were urging that the schoolchildren of America once more be made aware of the faith upon which our nation had been built.

Protestant churchmen, at a meeting of the National Council of Churches of Christ in the U.S.A., expressed it this way:

A way must be found to make the pupils of American schools aware of the heritage of faith upon which this nation was established. . . . On no account must an educational system which is permeated by the philosophy of secularism, something quite different from religious neutrality, be allowed to gain control of our public schools. . . . In some constitutional way provision should be made for the inclusion of the principles of religion . . . within the regular schedule of a pupil's working day.

About the same time, *American Education and Religion* quoted the following extract from *A Jewish Educator's View*, by Simon Greenberg:

The schools cannot be said to be teaching history at all, if they eliminate completely whole areas of vital human experience. Religion and religious institutions have been determining factors in the evolution of civilization. To omit a study of them in a course of history is to pervert history. The same is true of the relations of the great religious literary monuments to this history of literature generally. Nor can one honestly dodge the religious issue in the teaching of science and philosophy.

The Catholic bishops of the United States, at their annual meeting in Washington, made this statement:

Without religious education, moral education is impossible. . . . But if religion is important to good citizenship—and that is the burden of our national tradition—then the State must give recognition to its importance in public education.

Here was a marked unanimity of opinion expressed by representatives of the three outstanding religious groups of the United States. It seemed that the times once again presented an opportunity to amplify the Christopher idea.

So with Father Flannery's help I plunged back into a long period of research. Out of it came records of the countless instances of how the people of the United States had recognized the place of God in American life. I talked at length with teachers and administrators, and discussed the subject with authorities in education and its related fields. I studied the Supreme Court decisions touching this subject—decisions such as the following one which Justice Brewer wrote in 1892 after surveying some of our great national documents: "There is no dissonance in these Declarations. There is a universal language pervading them all, having one meaning. They affirm and reaffirm that this is a religious nation. These are not individual sayings, declarations of private persons. They are organic utterances. They speak the voice of the entire people."

The finished manuscript ran some ninety thousand words, all of which went to emphasize the need and obligation to bring back into our schools a better-balanced curriculum— one which would include, not exclude, the teaching of the spiritual roots and traditions of America. Though highlighting outstanding events and documents, it pointed out that fundamental spiritual values have always been assumed and accepted in our heritage and that an adequate understanding and respect for them is an essential requisite for the complete training and education of "All God's Children." The book was published under this title by Doubleday in the autumn of 1953. Among the many favorable comments it received was the following from J. Edgar Hoover, Director of the Federal Bureau of Investigation: "It is the obligation of each generation to transmit to its progeny those spiritual values and religious essentials which have been so vital a part of its heritage. In *All God's Children*, Father Keller vividly and concretely portrays this responsibility to our youth."

Dean Carl W. Ackerman, of the Graduate School of Journalism at Columbia University, said that it "throws light on the spiritual ideals and zeal of those who founded our schools and colleges. It lights a candle to reveal the spiritual source of our liberties."

It was gratifying to learn that this latest effort was as well received as previous Christopher books had been. Even now, fifteen years after *You Can Change the World* had been released, I frequently receive letters about one or the other of them. Many of these comments come from overseas, since several Christopher books have been translated into German, Spanish, Portuguese, Chinese, Yugoslav, and even into Tamil, an Indian dialect.

These letters enable us to keep a finger on the pulse of individuals in the marketplace, which always has been the lifeblood of Christopher work. They often provide the content for books, letters, broadcasts, and *News Notes*. These contacts are also a wonderful stimulus that keeps me looking for new ways and means of providing the basic spiritual motivation and down-to-earth suggestions that will help individuals to light their candle.

CHAPTER XVI

THE IMPACT OF *NEWS NOTES*

One of the many rewards of Christopher work is to see the fascinating ways in which individuals put the idea of a personal mission into practice. Retelling their stories has added a dynamic force to my talks, writings and broadcasts that mere theory could never give.

I remember one day, as I was about to do a network radio broadcast, I noticed that the program director was polite but obviously uninterested in what he probably regarded as one more routine job in his busy day.

While I was on the air, I recounted several instances of what people had done to light a candle. From time to time I stole a glance in his direction. With each story, he seemed to be listening more intently.

As soon as the broadcast was over, he came to me and said: "This Christopher idea has terrific possibilities. I'm not a Catholic myself but what you are driving at makes good sense. There's a bit of the missionary in every one of us. The trouble is that, so far, about the only ones working hard at it have been the fellows upsetting the world."

Time and again I hark back to this simple remark that expressed the Christopher idea in a nutshell: "There's a bit of the missionary in every one of us."

Months later, I was talking to a group of college students at a Newman Club meeting in Rochester, New York. I mentioned that the "bit of the missionary" could be developed in them if they would take up careers in the spheres of influence which affect everybody.

Less than a year afterwards, a young man dropped in at Christopher headquarters and told me a surprising story. He said that he and six of his senior classmates had been so struck by the emphasis on what they could do for the good of others that they had decided to give the "take-a-job-with-a-purpose" idea a try. Soon after graduation, my visitor said, he started to train as a newspaper writer. Four of the others were preparing to teach—two in high school and two in college. The remaining two had entered the seminary and were studying for the priesthood.

What could be better proof of the fact that an individual often needs only a passing word of encouragement to put his creative powers of mind, heart and soul into action!

Another instance of this came from a young man in Florida who wrote: "I have charge of all the music and entertainment at a hotel and beach club in Florida. Then an idea hit me. I went through all the music and comedy material and selected all the songs that I felt every member of the family could enjoy. That automatically eliminated all the smutty and suggestive items. For some weeks I was waiting for complaints —but they never came. In fact, you'd be surprised to see how many parents are bringing their children to dinner here."

Presenting these examples through Christopher talks, books and broadcasts has sparked many others to act in ways of their own choosing. The use of each medium has a unique value. But if one means of promotion had to be singled out, it would have to be the *Christopher News Notes*. Through the years they have proved to be the most effective way to stimulate and sustain an apostolic sense of purpose and direction among large numbers of people. This four-page pamphlet is mailed gratis eight times a year to a million and a quarter individuals.

Though more than 130 issues have been distributed, the format and type of content have remained practically the same as the first one I sent to a small group of interested friends in May 1946.

The bulletin is limited to approximately 3,000 words—or the equivalent of about ten double-spaced typewritten pages. It is purposely kept brief to catch the interest of busy people. But keeping the *Notes* concise and to the point requires continual research, sorting of material, and meticulous filing before the actual writing can start.

Frankly speaking, I have never relished the task of this research, writing and rewriting. But even for a nonprofessional author like myself, the burden has become somewhat lighter, since the *Notes* have proved to be so effective in reminding people to be doers in our critical times, rather than passive spectators.

From the very outset, it was apparent that if the *News Notes* were to hit their mark, they would have to deal with everyday human problems. Merely bemoaning defects in an abstract manner would not do the trick. The contents would have to suggest realistic, Christlike ways to bring about solutions.

A brief look at one of the issues that was titled "Twelve Ways to Improve Any Organization," may give some idea of why and how themes are chosen and developed.

There are some three million organizations of all types in the United States today. Since most individuals are involved in one way or another with a civic, fraternal, political, social or religious group, I felt that this topic was one that would be of interest to a wide audience.

It struck me that failure on the part of the average member to take an active part has caused many an organization to bog down. In some cases this omission has opened the way to serious abuses and has allowed the leadership to go by default to those who may be either incapable, disinterested, corrupt or downright subversive.

But I was equally convinced that each group is capable of great good if the members strive conscientiously to see that their particular association serves a high and noble purpose.

While anxious to be helpful, I realized there was a lot I didn't know about the subject. So for well over three months I delved into books, articles, and pamphlets in search of every possible item that would point out ways and means through which individuals could bring the missing ingredient back into their organizations, and shift from negative to positive in both attitude and action.

In addition to reading, I talked with many people who had extensive experience in church societies, club work, civic and school associations, trade unions, business groups and fraternal organizations. Each one contributed some bit of valuable information.

When all the material had been assembled, the next step was to study and sort it. Reducing a few thousand items to the 3,000-word limit of the *News Notes* was a formidable and challenging job, to say the least. Many important points could scarcely be touched. But this had a certain advantage. It forced me to be selective and to highlight only the most significant items, those that would hopefully spark readers to action.

This issue of *News Notes* was divided into twelve sections. In each one, only broad over-all suggestions were submitted, leaving the reader to decide for himself the specific "when, where and how" and to apply them in his particular circumstances.

One section was entitled "Live Up to Your Obligations." It

is typical of the general makeup of this issue and reads as follows:

Whatever your organization may be, it adds up to nothing more or less than one individual like you, over and over again. In short, *you* are the organization. What you do, or fail to do, can therefore help or hurt its worthy objectives.

Because you, personally and individually, are so important, make it your business to:

a) Be more than a "joiner." Membership confers rights, but it also imposes responsibilities.

b) Stir up rank and file members to recognize the importance of their personal participation.

c) Attend meetings faithfully and take an active interest in proceedings.

d) Work to eliminate unnecessary "red tape" and tedious procedures, which bore the average member and discourage attendance at meetings.

e) Think for yourself. Don't be a rubber stamp.

f) Work for the best interests of the entire membership, not a select few.

g) If you are in a minority trying to push good ideas, remember God blesses perseverance! As a member of the loyal opposition, you can serve a most useful purpose.

h) Improve your own ability and effectiveness. Learn the elementary principles of parliamentary law.

i) Develop the habit of getting all the facts, thinking things through, speaking on your feet and discussing issues in a logical way.

In addition to the million and a quarter copies sent to our regular mailing list, requests came in for four hundred thousand reprints of this particular issue of *News Notes*. Such interest not only indicated that the preparatory work had been worthwhile, but it also was the main reason we followed up a few months later with an issue on a related category, "How Parliamentary Law Protects You."

A mere listing of some of the titles of past *News Notes* may indicate the way each one tried to show individuals how to integrate divine values into the running of human affairs:

> Love People and Change the World
> Gear Yourself to a Fast-changing World
> Fifteen Ways to Strengthen Your Government
> Tips for Teen-agers
> Seven Ways to Overcome Communism
> How to Be a Leader
> Sixteen Tips for Potential Writers
> How to Strengthen Your Schools
> How to Become an Effective Speaker
> Fifteen Tips for Parents
> How to Write Effective Letters

Material is continually being collected for future issues. Countless file drawers and boxes are filled with notes, letters and clippings. Sometimes it's years before a particular item is used. As a result, not too much finds its way into the waste-basket, to the regret of some "spring-cleaning-minded" individuals around the office!

Despite the $40,000 cost involved in the printing, handling and mailing of each issue of the *News Notes*, they have always been sent free of charge to any adult requesting them. This goes back to my original conviction that many "doers" cannot be "donors." Because every facet of Christopher development has been based on voluntary participation, we ask that no one send us names unless such individuals have specifically asked for Christopher literature.

Requests for quantities of fifty, a hundred, and even thousands of copies of various issues come from individuals, schools, business organizations, trade unions, clubs, and a wide variety of other groups.

Besides these conventional outlets, unusual ingenuity has

been used to distribute the *Notes*. For instance, one dairyman includes a copy in all his egg deliveries; a trade union distributes them to its members; a fruit-cake manufacturer puts a copy in each package; a haberdasher slips the *News Notes* into the pockets of all the men's jackets in his store; the management of a large metropolitan hotel distributes them along with paychecks to employees; a salesman for kitchenware puts an issue in each outgoing order; and several companies include a copy with their bills. One man in Southern California, in asking for a monthly supply, wrote: "I would like to start by ordering two hundred copies which we (my wife and I) will display at our little hamburger stand." These instances and many more are a great tribute to individuals who take it upon themselves to light a candle without any urging on our part.

The reactions of the public are always an interesting measure of the effectiveness of almost any work, and I am continually learning from the thousand pieces of mail that come in every day. Those that refer to the *News Notes* naturally stimulate me to add greater impact to both their content and presentation.

A young woman in Santa Monica, California, wrote to tell us that she had been a secretary, but having been prodded by the *News Notes*, had entered college to study for teaching credentials. Another woman, who was already teaching in Salem, Oregon, said she wanted to receive the *News Notes* so that she could help her students "see the greatness of their lives." A non-Catholic professor at a southern university penned these lines: "Many thanks for the *News Notes*—I find ideas in them that enrich my teaching."

Students, too, often write to tell us their reactions. A young man in Ireland asked us to send him twenty copies, instead of one, so that he could give nineteen to his friends whom, he expected, would turn them over to their friends. "What I like best," he said, "is the way you quote the Gospel and the

Epistles and Holy Scripture along with what you have to say. I also like the way you give examples of what people are doing. It helps me work out what I could be doing, too, as well as giving good example.

"Your movement could do a lot of good in college. I am convinced of this. I don't think students realize what you realize, that good standards of ideas will prevail only as long as there are enough people to constantly put them forward. If these default, then the other lads come in. . . ."

From Ireland back to Rhode Island and the radio broadcaster who is trying to "light one little candle in the darkness" by featuring a blend of quality music, from the finer "pops" to the classics on his midnight-to-5:00 A.M. program.

In still another field, a Massachusetts trade union representative is a typical example of how individuals plunge into the thick of things when they realize that the opportunity to do something positive can and should be grasped. He said: "Since no one else seemed to have any interest in the position, I picked up the banner" in hopes of "promoting harmony between management and employees."

Furthering practical interest in government at all levels has always been a major part of the Christopher thesis. Two letters I received from individuals who had actually become involved on an elective level are similar, but with an interesting contrast.

A Congressman in Washington, D.C., said: "The Christophers got me started. I decided I should do something for my country. Now I'm in the House of Representatives." Not all who get a push from the Christopher formula win the office they seek, but few regret trying. Not long ago a man from Ohio told us that he had missed out in the election but: "Even though I lost, I made a good showing and found the experience challenging, gratifying and fruitful. I have no regrets and may even run again in two years."

A young man in Seattle, Washington, crystallized the idea that the Christopher movement is endeavoring to promote when he wrote: "After reading the *News Notes*, it seems any ordinary guy can't be lazy any more."

Receiving such reactions could not help but be a continuing challenge to reach more and more individuals. The results that come from such efforts are both heartening and a stimulating reminder of future possibilities.

One of the most gratifying effects of the Christopher approach is the attraction it has for many who have become weak in the practice of their religion or who have drifted away from it altogether.

A priest in Texas sent us a note about a radio performer who had received favorable comments about his program since he had tried to incorporate Christopher material in his broadcasts. The note went on to say: "His acquaintance with the movement has made him take his religion more seriously. Before he started to read Christopher material, he very seldom was receiving Communion, perhaps once or twice a year. He is now a daily communicant and that is all due to the influence of the Christophers."

Somewhat akin to this was the experience of a man in Minneapolis, Minnesota. He credited the *News Notes* with getting him by an emotional crisis and starting him on "the long and painful course which led me back into the Catholic Church after twenty years out of it."

Equally gratifying is the interest shown by leaders of other churches. One of the most unique tributes appeared in the weekly bulletin of a Methodist church in Southern California. The pastor wrote:

"As you unfold this issue of your church paper, you'll find a copy of *Christopher News Notes*. This movement of the Christophers is a very, very fine movement, in my opinion. Its purpose is to put dedicated Christian people into active positions of leadership in those vital areas of 1) government, 2) education, 3) literature, 4) entertainment, and 5) labor relations. . . . Ours could be a Christian nation in fact, as well as in name, if leaders in these crucial areas of American life were dedicated to Christ and His way of life above all else.

"This is such an all-important goal that we must not let the Roman Catholic Church monopolize the privilege of converting America. . . .

"As a Protestant leader, I would never 'fight' the Roman Catholic people in this exceptionally fine purpose; I would rather join them. I suggest that each reader . . . send in for this monthly *News Notes*."

Reactions such as these indicate the great potential in the simple idea that everyone can and should do something to change the world for the better.

Now and then through the years I've wondered what course my life might have taken had I been sent, as I once had confidently hoped, to do missionary work in some distant land. Yet, in a very real sense, God has made it possible—through the Christopher movement—for me to go to many villages and many cities in many lands.

A sampling of the mailbag can be a world tour. One letter from India read: "To put our impressions of the Christophers in the modern monosyllabic way of speech: it's 'just great'— not insofar as it embodies novel ideas and startling catch phrases, but because it has given the wonderful idea of Christian leadership a rollicking boost-up by resolving it down to the level of the common man so that he is raised up and above the monotony of a seemingly purposeless existence. That's what has enthused us all."

A request arrived from Formosa not long ago asking permission to translate the *Notes* into Chinese. Here's an excerpt from that letter: "It would be wonderful to have them appearing monthly in a Chinese edition, for every issue is a mine of short, concrete, concise ideas—precious 'scintilla,' spreading light, inspiration, courage, and stimulating the reader (whoever he may be) to light his candle for a better world."

Similar correspondence has also come in recently from the Fiji Islands, Peru, Japan, Indonesia, the Philippines, Tanganyika, England, Germany, Korea, Ghana, Malaya, Burma, New Zealand, Chile, Yugoslavia, Australia, Borneo, Mexico, Uganda, Venezuela and Basutoland.

These letters confirm my original hope and conviction that the Christopher movement can serve a worthwhile purpose in fostering a personal sense of mission in fields afar as well as in the homeland. They also bring fresh evidence that my dream of being a missioner in the fields afar has partially come true.

CHAPTER XVII

WHO PROVIDES THE MONEY?

One standard question that never fails to come up in discussions about the Christophers is: "Who pays the bills?" The answer has always been the same—anyone who wishes to make a voluntary contribution.

When I told some close friends that I planned to start and operate the movement under a policy of no memberships, no branches, no dues, and no fund-raising drives beyond a once-a-year announcement of needs, they were frankly skeptical. They not only regarded it as a vague and impractical approach for a long-term basis, but were convinced the movement would scarcely get started without some assured source of income.

But despite their misgivings, I was sincerely convinced that if we spent the major portion of our time and effort stimulating the "doers," the Lord would provide the "donors." I believed this policy would bring a special blessing on the work. I also felt it would gradually attract financial support from individuals who wished to become "partners" in a venture they felt was furthering the ideas they believed important, but which they couldn't circulate widely on their own.

In maintaining this policy, I have gone so far as to stop several collections that friends have initiated for Christopher support. Once, after returning from a visit to Houston, Texas, I heard that a very thoughtful friend had started to conduct his own fund-raising drive in behalf of the Christophers. I phoned him right away to explain as tactfully as I could that it would be best if he didn't pursue this tack. He said that it was the first time he had ever done anything like this of his own accord and couldn't figure out why in the world I wanted him to stop; after all, the money he could collect would further many of our projects.

I certainly appreciated his initiative and enterprise and didn't want to offend him. But I tried to point out that those whom he contacted would probably give because he asked them to, and not because they were particularly "sold" on the worth of Christopher work. I assured him that if people were really interested, they would give on their own.

At the time of our conversation, he wasn't too convinced of the soundness of my argument. But since then, he has agreed that it was a valid one. And he has subsequently told numerous people of Christopher work without "passing the hat."

This method of encouraging Christopher friends to "announce" our work and needs to their friends has been most fruitful. They spread the idea but, at the same time, point out that support for the work should come voluntarily.

A situation similar to the one in Houston came up once while I was in Milwaukee, Wisconsin. After giving a talk there to about four hundred people, I returned to my seat in the front row of the auditorium so that the chairman could wind up the meeting. To my surprise, he began his closing remarks by announcing that, although he knew the Christophers did not ask for collections, he thought an exception could be made. And then and there he asked the ushers to go down the aisles. I didn't want to seem ungrateful for this generous gesture, but I still thought it wise not to deviate from our policy. So, back I went to the stage to state my case. After explaining the "why and wherefore" of what probably would seem like a strange request, I respectfully asked that the ushers refrain from taking up the collection.

Later, as we were leaving the auditorium, a woman who had been in the audience came up to speak to me. She said she had been impressed by the Christopher approach in regard to financial support, as well as by my admission that it had certain drawbacks—such as giving the idea that we really didn't need funds. Nevertheless, she said that it struck her as very sound and would undoubtedly prove itself in the long run.

Even close friends sometimes wonder at the Christopher financial outlook. I remember a conversation with one man who asked what money we had and what we expected to take in during the next few months. I had to confess that we didn't have too much and that I had no idea what the future would bring. His only comment was that he would have a bad case of ulcers if he had to operate this way.

Fortunately, ulcers have never materialized and the success that this theory of voluntary help has had in practice is evidence, to me at least, of the hand of God in this work. He has never put the Christophers on "easy street" and we have often had to curtail or postpone projects for lack of funds. But since the start of the work eighteen years ago, we have always been able to keep ahead of the bill collectors and meet the budget, which runs as high as $70,000 a month.

The *News Notes* account for the biggest single expenditure —$40,000 per issue, or $320,000 annually. Television films and radio recordings run a close second. Although the nearly 3,000 different stations that regularly schedule Christopher programs donate free air time, worth at least $8,000,000 a year, it costs us close to $250,000 to produce and distribute the films and transcriptions.

These two figures alone are ample proof that, although

there is no formal fund drive, there is certainly a need for financial support both for current and new undertakings.

Many persons volunteer aid because they realize that the need for donors is purposely "soft-pedaled" in order to focus attention on the more important need for "doers."

"I am always impressed by the lack of appeal for funds in your *News Notes*," an interested person in Providence, Rhode Island, wrote. "This very omission is a reminder your work must be financed. I enclose my offering."

I never cease to thank God for numerous letters like that which come in each week bringing help for Christopher work.

The personal sacrifice that many of the gifts represent is heartening proof that individuals really and truly wish to help. For example, one lady walked to work every day for two weeks so she could send her carfare to help defray Christopher expenses. Another sent us $2.00 which she had earned babysitting. From Knapp, Wisconsin, we received this note: "We are not able to make a large contribution, but we are enclosing a check for $11.80 which we received for a calf. Hope to raise a calf each year for the Christophers as our small part in this wonderful work you are doing."

A friend from Brooklyn, New York, told us: "Ordinarily I would be embarrassed to send only one dollar but you make me feel as though it would help." A Cleveland, Ohio, donor worked out this system: "I will pay you 10¢ a day for a year —365 days. Please find enclosed my check for $36.50. Thank you for allowing me to help." And, attached to a $28 check from Long Island was this delightful note: "One dollar for each year of a wonderful marriage."

Some donors contribute what they can regularly each month, but the majority participate on a once-a-year basis. Occasionally we receive large gifts that are not only generous but sometimes unique. I especially remember one for $5,000, sent by a woman who did not belong to any church.

"I know you say," she wrote, "that you always trust to the angels for the funds you need for the Christophers, but this time one of the 'devils' came through."

Our most generous benefactor happens to be an Episcopalian. Since 1948, his yearly gift has been the largest that we have received from any one source. This brief comment accompanied his first donation:

"While I am a non-Catholic, I so earnestly believe in the great work that the Catholic Church is doing through the Christopher movement that I would like to contribute a little to its effort."

Oftentimes, individuals who are unable to give funds themselves arouse the interest of others who can. Such was the case with a young secretary in Chicago. She sent a copy of our *News Notes* to a friend who worked as secretary to a Pittsburgh businessman. When the enclosure arrived, her employer happened to be in Florida, but the Pittsburgh secretary was so struck by the message in the *Notes* that she enclosed them in her next letter to him.

After the gentleman had read them and showed them to his wife, she said: "Here is a group that is really trying to improve things. Let's send them a thousand dollars."

The candle lit by those two secretaries has continued to burn brightly. The businessman and his wife have generously contributed to Christopher work ever since.

In the past few years, another source of support has come through more frequent remembrances in wills. It is a consolation to know that individuals who participated in Christopher work during life wish to assure its continuation in this way.

In the same interest of continuity, a few friends have made contributions of cash, stock or real estate that have been set aside in a small endowment fund. In doing so, they have pointed out that various good works have often been crippled because no provision has been made for unforeseen emergencies and critical periods. They feel that a special fund which eventually could meet 10 per cent of our operating costs would be a wise safeguard for the future of the movement.

In 1959, a new financial undertaking loomed on the horizon. When I asked myself if I dared take it on, the answer came in the affirmative with that quotation which had seen me through many another venture: "For a web begun, God will supply the thread."

The "web" in this case was a permanent headquarters for Christopher work.

After fourteen years of trial, the widespread acceptance of the Christopher idea indicated that the movement was here to stay and should be geared to operate on a solid, efficient, long-range basis.

Actually, new quarters were a "must" for more than this reason. We were bursting at the seams in our rented space on the fourteenth floor of the Great Lakes Carbon Building at 18 East Forty-eighth Street, where Christopher operations had been underway for twelve years.

Purchasing a small building, however, was not something I could just go out and do. It was a move that called for both advice and permission.

First I spoke to Bishop John W. Comber, the Superior General of Maryknoll. He had been elected to this post in 1956 after extensive missionary experience in Manchuria and Chile, as well as nine years as rector of the Maryknoll Seminary.

The interest and cooperation he has shown in Christopher efforts has meant a great deal to the development of the movement. As a matter of fact, he felt that some of the methods we would develop might be utilized in Maryknoll work. So he has invited me to attend monthly planning meetings at Maryknoll headquarters. The discussions of missionary promotion work have proved beneficial to both our efforts.

The Bishop's understanding of the importance of fostering a sense of personal mission among as many individuals as possible made him well disposed towards the plan that would put the Christopher movement on a more permanent basis.

Bishop Comber gave his approval to purchase a building for the Christophers on condition that I obtain formal permission from Cardinal Spellman, Archbishop of New York. Some years before, His Eminence had appointed Bishops Edward V. Dargin, John J. Maguire and John M. A. Fearns, along with Father Thomas A. Walsh of Maryknoll, to a special advisory committee to provide guidance for the Christopher movement. So I took the matter of a permanent center to them. They graciously gave me the clearance to look for and purchase a suitable building.

Now that I had the "go ahead," my next move was to put the quest in the hands of the Lord. I sent a letter to various convents throughout the country and asked the nuns to pray that we might secure a small, reasonably priced and well-located building.

The midtown Manhattan area still seemed to be the ideal spot. Within the radius of a few blocks are the national headquarters of broadcasting and motion picture companies, press associations, magazine and book publishers, advertising agencies, textbook companies and numerous other endeavors that, for better or worse, affect the political, educational, social and economic destiny of countless millions throughout the United States and over the world. By the grace of God, more than a few candles had already been lighted because the Christopher headquarters had been located in this vital district.

Wanting a small building in the heart of New York City is one thing. But finding it, along with the necessary purchase funds, is quite a different problem.

There was some advantage in having the area narrowed down, but it certainly didn't produce a magic solution. All the available buildings seemed to be out of our price range. Nevertheless, we kept looking.

After about a year, I discovered that the answer was right next door. The small building where I had set up the original Maryknoll office thirty years before was to be vacated by the Camp Fire Girls, who were moving to larger offices. In the early days, we had occupied only two rooms on the fifth floor of that building. But by 1960, all seven floors could be used to advantage.

Though it seemed like an ideal solution in many respects, it took a little time to iron out the difficulties that still existed —not the least of which was the $375,000, mostly in borrowed money, that was needed to purchase, alter and equip it.

I felt that any and all efforts to obtain it would be well worth it, since this center would suppy new impetus to our work. It would give us the needed room for our staff of forty, and also allow us to develop many projects that had been held up for lack of space.

The move to the new quarters was made on Saturday, January 9, 1960, in the midst of one of the season's coldest days. But thanks to the willing and able help of twenty husky teen-agers from local high schools, the big transfer of desks, typewriters, mimeograph machines, books, filing cases, packing cartons and office supplies was done all in one day.

By Monday morning, work was going on at the normal pace, with one noticeable difference—a quick look around the corner in the old quarters was all that was needed to take in every operation at a glance. Now the work was distributed over seven floors.

The seventh floor was turned over to meeting rooms, as well as storage space for books and literature that had formerly been lodged in a rented loft.

The research library, mimeograph machines and mailing department settled on the fifth and sixth floors.

The radio-TV operations moved into the fourth floor, where racks for the over four thousand half-hour and fifteen-minute TV programs now fill most of the wall space. Postmen come three times a day with large laundry-type bins, filled with more films to be processed and readied for shipment. The constant flow makes this one of the busiest Christopher departments.

The third floor houses the sponsor, order and filing departments. There is never a lull in activity here either. One project alone involves the fifty thousand yearly address changes for the million and more names on our mailing list. Since this is more or less the building's "central location," the whole staff assembles here every morning at nine o'clock to begin the day with a prayer for Christopher benefactors, a short rundown of highlights from the mailbag, or a report on undertakings that the Christopher staff has helped to make possible.

The second floor provides classroom space for our leadership course. Here, too, the *News Notes* are prepared, as well as books, programs and newspaper columns. It also provides space for my office and that of the assistant director, another Maryknoller, Father Richard Armstrong.

Bishop Comber generously assigned him to fill this spot. Fortunately for us, several other priests have spent varying periods of time at Christopher headquarters. Through the years, they have contributed a great deal to the development of Christopher work and have also worked out ways of incorporating certain facets of the idea into their own activities. In having a day-to-day association with Christopher doings, they have also become acquainted with the responsibilities of directing the movement so that its continuity will be assured.

Among the priests who have participated in this way are: Fathers Thomas Bresnahan of Detroit, Michigan; John Cra-

dick of St. Louis, Missouri; Prudencio Damboriena, S.J., of
Rome, Italy; Edward Flannery of Providence, Rhode Island;
Joseph Flynn of the Paulist Fathers; Robert Howes of
Worcester, Massachusetts; as well as Maryknoll Fathers
Walter Kelleher and Graham McDonnell.

The Christopher Award is another activity centered on the
second floor of our new building. In one form or another, the
awards have been presented every year since 1950.

They have been given to authors, producers and directors
in the communications media. The list of winners has frequently included names that are well known to the general
public. But just as often, those singled out have worked behind the scenes and are best known to their fellow workers
in the industry. In each instance the decision of the judges
has been based on these considerations: a) The content of
each work must be of high quality, with emphasis on *what* is
said, not only on *how* it is said; b) It must be suitable for the
entire family; c) It should be of interest to the many, not
merely the few; d) A citation does not mean perfection, but
it does signify creditable effort and results.

Through the years, the announcement of the awards has
varied from an annual one to a semiannual or quarterly release. Occasionally, presentations have been made at a formal
reception. But more often, the recipient is notified by letter,
and a news release then carries the public notice.

But whatever form the announcement takes, it always
stresses that the Christopher Award should be regarded as
simply a "pat on the back" and a reminder of the power for
good that those in the creative fields can exert by using their
God-given talent affirmatively.

Following through on this theme, each winner is given a
bronze plaque inscribed with his name and the quotation
which we long ago adopted as the Christopher motto: "It
is better to light one candle than to curse the darkness."

The reactions of those receiving the awards have been most interesting. A writer for a large weekly magazine, for example, wrote:

This is my twentieth anniversary as a writer. It has not been an easy road, and I have wondered often if the compensation was equal to the periodic disappointment and heartache. Now, at last, at this milestone, I can look over my shoulder and smile. Your Christopher Award has made all of it seem very worthwhile.

The producer of a successful television program made this comment:

How deeply grateful I am to the Christophers for this particular honor. You describe it as a little "pat on the back." In my case the pat went clear to my soul and left there a glowing hope that perhaps in some small way I have been able to make a tiny part of my bright dream for television come true. You may be assured that any show with which I have any connection will be built with this same constructive and positive purpose as its cornerstone.

The awards, like every aspect of Christopher work, have a specific purpose—to remind as many individuals as possible of the responsibility each has to "change the world for the better." In each case, they honor those who have made their contribution through media that touch and shape the lives of millions of people.

We have had to put off plans temporarily for using the first floor of our new Christopher center, as the space is now occupied by a small restaurant. Its owners had a long-term lease with a few years to run when we took over the building.

As soon as they find a suitable new location, we intend to use this area to receive the ever increasing number of visitors who come to find out more about Christopher work or to pick up books and *News Notes*. The added space will also accommodate various developments of the Christopher leadership program.

In the two and a half years since we have been in the new location, all facets of our work have grown steadily. Of course, it will take time to complete payments on our new building, but as in all our Christopher projects, we do our best to make ends meet and then "leave it to the angels." Thanks to the Lord's blessings and the generosity of numerous friends who have been "doers" and "donors," the Christopher idea continues to reach new and wider horizons.

CHAPTER XVIII

TRAINING FOR LEADERSHIP

One of the first projects that came off the planning board when we settled into our new quarters was the development of a leadership program.

As Christopher work progressed through the years, I became more and more convinced of the need for training in this area. The necessity of doing it through formalized courses was pointed up when I saw what the Communists accomplished through the Jefferson School of Social Sciences, which opened in New York in February 1944.

According to the Communist *Daily Worker* of January 3, 1949, the school trained fifty thousand people in the first five years of its existence—an average of ten thousand a year.

I was fortunate enough to talk with a number of persons who, out of curiosity, had attended the school. Their explanations of how the instructors stressed both purpose and direction, no matter what the subject, made me very much aware of the threat that this training center represented.

"What we give you," they said, "does not belong to you alone. Don't keep it to yourself. Get out and spread it. Don't accept just any kind of job. Take one that counts—one where your ideas will have some effect, and where you can influence others. Let other people take the ordinary jobs, but be particular yourselves. Get on the staff of a college—on a board of education—in a government office—in a labor union—on a radio station—in writing or publishing—or anything else that will make it possible for you to influence large numbers of people."

In addition to the regular subjects, the students were given direct and indirect lessons on how to apply and integrate Marxism into whatever field they entered. Those who received such preparation and training often developed a dynamic zeal that made them effective instruments of Communist philosophy.

Thirty-seven of these Communist schools were eventually opened in the United States. Under the guise of all sorts of attractive names (many of them with patriotic connotations), they not only indoctrinated their own followers but misled many who were sincerely searching for information, training, and motivation.

Their activities made it more and more apparent that nations, and even the world, would be won or lost in proportion to the quality of leadership developed and exerted by people with sound ideas.

Nikolai Lenin himself called attention to this when he said: "If there had been in Petrograd in 1917 a group of only a few thousand men who knew what they wanted, we would never have come to power in Russia."

As I watched and thought about what the Communists were accomplishing for destructive ends, it struck me that the leadership-training idea should be used to even greater advantage by the followers of the Lord.

They would, of course, find that true leadership implies hardship, misunderstanding, personal risk and sometimes personal loss. But I felt that anyone willing to try would find their troubles small in comparison to the sense of personal fulfillment and achievement for the good of all—especially if they kept in mind what the Leader of leaders Himself said:

"He who would save his life will lose it; but he who loses his life for My sake will find it." (Matthew 16:25)

Lack of time, space and money had been deterrents in setting up any formal training arrangement in the first years of Christopher work. The best I could do in the beginning was to hammer away at the idea in *News Notes* and talks. Even the few suggestions I was able to make in this way on how and why to communicate good ideas seemed to come as a happy surprise to most people.

Many seemed to be uncomfortably aware that they weren't really doing their share in their homes, churches, schools, community, country and, ultimately, the world. But their inaction was not so much a matter of "not wanting to" as "not knowing how."

Several groups in the country, notably the Gabriel Richard Institute of Detroit, Michigan, worked out effective programs, partially based on Christopher material. They succeeded in encouraging numerous persons to become active in various spheres of influence.

The results of these formalized programs, along with the reactions I had received from people in all walks of life convinced me that the time had finally come for us to work out a leadership formula that could be used on a wide scale throughout this country as well as overseas. Its fundamental aim would be to help people of all occupations use their God-given talents to shape the critical trends of our times by communicating their ideas more effectively.

A year or more of actual experience with individuals in a classroom setting would, I felt, give us the necessary "know how" to draw up a handbook that could be used by individuals or groups anywhere.

In setting up the courses, we had the competent assistance of Mrs. June Guncheon Vajda. For the previous ten years she had taught employers and employees in the New York area the basic techniques of communicating ideas. Her experience in both the planning stages and in training the men and women who volunteered to become instructors proved invaluable.

The function of the Christopher leadership instructors is to guide and encourage the participants while drawing attention to basic leadership techniques. They also keep sessions moving along in a brisk, orderly fashion, and moderate the proceedings to avoid lengthy discussions. The capable and generous cooperation of each one serving in this capacity has been no small factor in the success of the courses at Christopher headquarters.

Classes are limited to twenty-five or thirty persons. This provides each with an opportunity to give at least two short talks at each session and thus "learn by doing." It also allows time for constructive comments from the instructors on how to become more forceful communicators of good ideas at home, on the job and in various types of meetings and groups.

We have found that best results are achieved when the course runs for seven once-a-week sessions of three hours each. Since there is a planned progression from one lesson to the next, we stress the importance of attending every session.

In the opening lesson, each participant takes the first few steps towards gaining self-confidence. He stands before the group and gives a two-minute impromptu talk about himself, his work or family, as well as his reasons for taking the leadership course. It takes well over an hour for all members of the group to give their first brief talk. All during these introductory speeches, there is keen interest on the part of the other participants because they see that everyone is equally fearful and lacking in experience. Later, they stand up before the group again and talk for one minute about any item in one of the *Christopher News Notes*. The progress of most individuals in a single lesson is truly remarkable.

As the seven-week course progresses, lessons are devoted to such topics as: how to begin and end a talk; how to gather facts and present them effectively; how to add clarity and interest; and how to convince and persuade. Since a great percentage of most people's "public speaking" is done in groups and organizations, without advance planning and notes, separate lessons are devoted to playing an effective role in meetings, and to speaking on the spur of the moment.

Thirty persons arrived one evening in October, 1961, for the opening of the first of these courses. "First nights" of any kind always carry a certain sense of excitement and anticipation, and that evening was no exception. It was a gratifying experience for those who participated as well as for those who had made the preliminary arrangements. Seeing a long-cherished hope become a reality was particularly memorable for me. As I met the participants coming in and later observed their "performances" from the back of the room, I was more convinced than ever that a leadership-training program could be one of the most effective projects undertaken by the Christophers.

It is fascinating to watch an individual who realizes for the first time that he is actually capable of standing up and expressing the ideas he feels are important. When that bit of leadership is discovered and unlocked, it is a stimulating moment for both speaker and audience.

Many who were there that first night had never gotten up in front of an audience before and, quite naturally, they were ill-at-ease and frightened at the prospect of speaking on their feet. But the case of one 43-year-old truck driver typifies the transformation that can take place even on the first try.

When he arrived, a little late, he frankly admitted he had walked around the block a few times to get up enough courage to come in. He wanted to know if he could just sit in on the first session without getting up to speak.

We have never favored "auditing" and we don't encourage people to register for the course unless they are willing and determined to participate in all seven sessions.

But in this case I felt it was wise to make an exception, and it proved to be providential.

During the first part of the evening, he did sit on the side lines of the group. But as person after person, just as inexperienced and nervous as himself, went to the front of the room and talked for two minutes about themselves, their occupations or family, and their reasons for taking the leadership course, he was visibly impressed.

When everyone else had spoken, the truck driver raised his hand and asked if he might also say a few words.

He went to the front of the room and with remarkable ease and clarity told the audience his name and talked about his job.

Then he calmly continued: "I belong to the Teamsters Union. I know I have good ideas and I know I should be bringing them into my union meetings. But I am not doing this because I don't know how. That's why I am here—to learn how to speak up in my own union."

This man was quite obviously surprised to find that he could give outward expression to his inner convictions, and in this he is typical of the majority of those who have taken the Christopher leadership course. When they come on that first evening they are, for the most part, isolated individuals. Often, they don't know anyone else in the group and are fearful and mousy. But once they take that initial plunge and discover that they, along with everyone else in the group, have the ability to stand up and be heard, a sharing of ideas and a positive kinship develops. Seldom, if ever, have many of them had a chance to speak before a more sympathetic and helpful group of people than their fellow participants. Many of them told me it was unlike any experience they had had before. This development is not due to what I or anyone else has given them, but what they have done for themselves.

I cannot help but think of the difference it could make in the world if millions more would take the few necessary steps that would help them switch from being passive onlookers to articulate transmitters of dynamic ideas.

Soon we were conducting three courses on weekday evenings from six to nine o'clock. Hundreds of individuals from many backgrounds and walks of life have attended. Among them are lawyers, bank clerks, Cuban and Hungarian refugees, trade unionists, foreign students, business executives, secretaries, teen-agers, housewives, teachers, missionary students, airline workers, salesmen, college students, police officers and firemen, as well as a research director, detective, accountant, engineer, telephone supervisor, policewoman and bookkeeper. They have come to us through newspapers, "friend to friend" recommendations, or Christopher literature.

The reasons they give for taking the course speak for themselves. One man put it this way: "I often think how effective I could be if only I could communicate. All my good ideas stick in my throat whenever I get up at a meeting. I sit down feeling like a fool."

Over and over again, their remarks show that there is a growing awareness and desire on the part of individuals to improve themselves so that they can be a greater force for good. Many are frustrated because they don't have the simple tools that would enable them to share their ideas. As one woman described it: "On my way home, I think of all the things I should have said. I'd like to see whether I can get up enough courage to speak at the right time."

One man had a valid if amusing reason for signing up. He told us: "Whenever we go to parent-teacher meetings, my wife nudges me all during the meeting to get up and say something. . . . I'm taking the course in self-defense."

The awareness that we are playing for big stakes was evident in this remark made by a graduate of the University of Havana: "When I was studying, the Communist students there boasted they would one day take over our country. They said they would surely win because they worked hard while we played. To our sorrow we found out how right they were. I hope this leadership course will help me make up for mistakes in the past."

The importance of developing a facility for self-expression was realized for a different reason by a mother who said: "My children are in high school and they can express their ideas better than I can express mine. I'm embarrassed as a parent, so I decided to do something about it."

Many are giving serious attention to the conviction that each one can and must make a constructive contribution to the world. One young lady admitted: "I often wonder whether I'm doing enough by just working. I really worry about the fact that I don't seem to be making any contribution to society. I don't think I am helping others. Maybe this course can help me to do that in some way."

At the start of each course that is given here at the Christophers, I usually give a few words of greeting before the instructors take over. I often use this quotation from Aristotle:

> It is not enough to know what to say;
> It is necessary also to know how to say it.

To me it is very indicative of the aim of the course. And it is a point I have tried to keep in mind ever since Leo McCarey reminded me of its importance during the shooting of that first Christopher film.

We do not expect to "graduate" polished orators. But we do hope that by the end of the seven sessions, participants will have taken the first important steps towards leadership.

One woman, for instance, who is a lawyer by day, took the course and later became an instructor. She said that the spirit and help she gained from others at the leadership course have aided her in her work to a remarkable degree. Another person said that he was finding it much easier to get his ideas across to his wife and children.

Many have gone into their church and community organizations with renewed vigor and welcome results. One man, for example, has succeeded in encouraging others to join him in straightening out a vital school-board question in his area.

Going even further, another man ran for Congress and still another went to work in the State Department. Many, too, have started their own courses, and in so doing are instrumental in bringing basic leadership training to much wider horizons.

These incidents, while not remarkable in themselves, are repeated by countless individuals. As such, they would seem to be eloquent proof that once people are given a few essential tools and a basic spiritual motivation, they are well on the way to becoming effective communicators of good ideas at home and on the job, as well as in church, civic, educational, labor and social activities.

As our work in this area of training became more widely known, requests for material began coming to us from all over this country and other parts of the world.

A letter from the Philippines contained this disturbing but hopeful statement: "There is a disastrous lack of leadership here. So much could be done if the talents of so many qualified Filipinos were put to work."

Comments such as this, which grew into the thousands, stepped up work on the handbook that had been part of the original aim in setting up the leadership classes.

And so, *How to Be a Leader—by Communicating Your*

Ideas was published in January of 1963. Any individual or group is free to set up a leadership course and use the handbook as a working guide. The responsibility for starting and conducting such a course rests completely with its sponsors or members, and we always ask them not to call it a Christopher leadership course since our strict policy is not to authorize any Christopher groups, branches or representatives.

The handbook includes forty pages of guidance notes for those who assume the role of instructor. They do not need previous training. The practical suggestions running through the book are those that have "proved themselves" in the courses we have conducted at Christopher headquarters.

Novices at public speaking are not the only ones who have found the suggestions valuable. Even after years of being "on my feet" in front of an audience, these tips have proved to be most helpful in my own talks.

In communicating, one of the points we try to emphasize, first and foremost, is the need to have a liking for people. Whether talking to one person or a thousand, it takes just a second to realize whether a person is eager to share good ideas or whether his words are merely coming from the lips. Love of people for love of God is an essential quality of a true leader.

Over and over again, we have found that, once individuals adopt this all-embracing attitude, they want to participate and not be only spectators—be it at home, at work or in any organization to which they belong. They want to make their voices heard, realizing that unexpressed ideas are "of no more value than the kernels in a nut before it is cracked."

Quite automatically, they also try to understand the other person's point of view and aren't tempted to use sarcasm, barbed remarks or personal insults to get their ideas across. It doesn't take long for any of us to realize that this approach accomplishes nothing aside from indicating personal weakness.

Understanding the other person's point of view also turns most people into good listeners. There is lots to be learned from the thoughts and ideas of others. This was put very well by Epictetus when he said: "Nature has given to man one tongue, but two ears, that we may hear from others twice as much as we speak."

Most people, myself included, are a bit nervous when they speak before a group, but the course points out how a little fear can be turned into an asset. For one thing, it sharpens ideas and keeps a speaker on his toes. Once individuals realize that they can be God's instruments in bringing helpful ideas to others, they automatically focus attention on what they are trying to say, and the fear of being misunderstood or laughed at seems to fade into the background. I have often found that saying a simple prayer like the following before a talk provides that needed Christlike calm: "Be in my heart and on my lips, O Lord, that I may worthily and fittingly proclaim Your truth."

This spirit of calm, plus clear, sound thinking, shows up in a speaker's tone of voice and facial expression, as well as in the rate at which he speaks and the degree of enthusiasm he puts into his talks.

This last quality is not to be confused with bombast, wild gestures or emotional display. It is rather a reflection of the meaning of the word *enthusiasm* itself, which comes from the Greek words "en" and "theos," translated as "in God." The divine spark will show through if a speaker really wants to communicate constructive ideas.

When we caution against wild gestures, it does not exclude using outward expressions such as a wave of the arm, a raising of the eyebrow, shrugging the shoulders or nodding the head. These all add dimension and inner conviction. Perhaps the most important thing in this category is "eye communication." It is far more than "eye contact" and really means talking with your eyes.

In different ways, each lesson touches on the important thought in these few lines:

> If wisdom's ways you wisely seek,
> Five things you will observe with care;
> Of whom you speak, to whom you speak,
> And how and when and where.

One direct outgrowth of this thought is learning how to think before speaking and taking a few seconds to organize thoughts, rather than blurting out a gush of words that don't know where they are going.

This naturally assumes that the speaker has information and ideas that should be put in order. Keeping informed is a key quality and not an easy one to acquire. It often means sacrificing leisure time, but anyone will be a more effective leader at home, on the job or in organizations if he keeps himself informed about local, national and international questions. Tearing out items in newspapers and magazines, and underscoring passages in books is a very practical way of keeping informed. Jotting ideas down on three-by-five slips of paper and keeping a little notebook have always proved helpful to me. And using some sort of file arrangement keeps facts and "slices of life" handy for preparing talks. This "ammunition" enables you to make your voice heard with much more certainty and conviction.

We also stress that having a lot of facts and information doesn't mean that when you speak in either a formal or impromptu manner you should forget about being brief and precise. We advise picking a point and getting to it—long and unnecessary explanations are boring for any audience. People are much more disposed to digest points that are presented economically, in short sentences and with well-selected words.

Most individuals want to be left with something to think about after a speech, but as one verse puts it, they would also say:

> I love a finished speaker;
> Oh yes, indeed I do.
> I don't mean one who's polished,
> I just mean one who's through.

Suggestions such as these are typical of the hundreds that run through the Christopher course. They are not the complete and only answer to leadership, to be sure, but when individuals try putting them to work in the heart of the marketplace, they often find they have the same leavening effect as a cake of yeast does when it is put into dough.

This Biblical analogy has always been a favorite of mine. Many years ago when I thought about using it in our *News Notes*, I talked with several people connected with the yeast industry to see if the likeness could be legitimately drawn.

I remember their rather surprised and amused reactions when I first mentioned this angle. But when I finished, they not only assured me that I was on the right track, but one man went so far as to say that he regarded his product with "new respect."

In further reading on the subject I found that, for centuries, the magic life-giving power of yeast had been a source of mystery and great speculation until 1857, when Louis Pasteur painstakingly and conclusively proved that the transforming properties of yeast stem from the fact that it is a living organism.

It was his experiments which demonstrated that a living thing must always be the starting point for the production of more living matter.

The comparison between yeast and the individual became

an obvious one: just as the "live" cake of yeast must be in the midst of inert dough to do its energizing work, so must the individual get his ideas into the marketplace if they are to do any good. Yeast affects nothing so long as it remains on the shelf in its wrapper.

It is always a source of great hope and inspiration for me to know that each person can act like a bit of "divine yeast." By developing his leadership potential, he can make a distinct contribution towards raising the level of the great spheres of influence that, for better or worse, affect every individual here and hereafter.

CHAPTER XIX

ONLY THE BEGINNING

A plane trip between New York and Los Angeles was the scene of an experience that once again indicated how surprised and pleased most people are when they realize that practically anyone can do something to blend the divine into the human.

The nonstop flight was crowded. By the time we were about to take off, all the seats were filled but one—and that was next to me. The last passenger aboard was a nattily dressed young man who had the look of a junior executive. Making his way down the aisle, he stopped where I was sitting. First he looked at me, and then at the empty seat. I got the impression that being next to a priest all the way to California was not his cup of tea. But since it was the only spot left, he had no choice.

I was on my way to the West Coast to film some programs for the Christopher television series, and I was already working on one of the scripts when he sat down.

We had scarcely gotten off the ground when my seat mate quite unexpectedly turned and said: "Of course, I don't believe in any religion. I'm an agnostic."

I passed over his remark as gently as I could, figuring that it would be better if he pursued the matter himself. I had met many persons like him before, and invariably found that they usually believe much more than they think they do.

Nothing more was said for about an hour. Then, as we

were flying over Indiana, he asked in a very friendly way what my work was.

I told him about my connection with the Christophers.

"I've heard about that idea," he nodded, "and it sounds pretty good. But just what is its objective?"

"All we're trying to do," I told him, "is to find as many people as possible to apply a little of the law and order of heaven to the running of things down here on earth."

His expression changed and he was almost enthusiastic when he replied: "Why that's a terrific idea!"

Long before we reached California it became quite evident that he was not nearly so much of an agnostic as he had imagined.

This hopeful, sobering experience left a deep impression on me. As I thought about it later, it seemed added evidence of the untold good that could result if enough followers of the Lord integrated divine love and truth into every segment of public and private life.

In its own contrasting way, an incident I heard about from one of our Maryknoll missioners when I was in the Orient over thirty years ago recalls the same point.

He told me that one bitterly cold day in Manchuria he met a withered old native woman dressed in rags and weak with hunger. When he led her to shelter and provided her with hot food, she was grateful but puzzled.

"Why do you bother with me when no one else cares?" she asked.

The priest explained a little about Christ's great command to go out over the whole world and help people, especially those who suffer.

"This Christ," the puzzled woman replied, "He cannot be long dead."

The missioner explained that He lived more than nineteen hundred years ago.

"Nineteen hundred years ago!" she said. "It was then that He commanded those who followed Him to spread this wonderful idea?"

The missioner nodded.

"Then where," the woman asked very slowly, "have His followers been for such a long time? Why haven't they done as He told them to do?"

It is plain in many ways that we are doing far from enough to blend the two great commandments of love into the mainstream of life, even though Jesus Christ made their interdependence quite clear in these three distinctions:

1. He began by saying: "This is the first commandment: Thou shalt love the Lord thy God with thy whole heart, and with thy whole soul, and with thy whole mind."

2. Then He immediately added: "And the second is like to this: Thou shalt love thy neighbor as thyself."

3. Finally, as if warning one and all not to tamper with the wholeness of this twofold divine formula, Christ concluded: "On these two great commandments depend the whole law and the prophets." (Matthew 22:37–40)

Overlooking the interlocking nature of these two commandments can, and has, caused great harm. This is exemplified in an item I have quoted many times. It originally appeared in the French Communist publication *Paix et Liberté* in 1957. It presented this taunting rebuke:

The gospel is a much more powerful weapon for the renovation of society than our Marxist view of the world. Yet it is we who shall conquer you in the end.

Of our salaries and wages we keep only what is absolutely necessary and the rest we give up for propaganda purposes.

To this same propaganda we also devote our leisure time and part of our vacation.

You, however, give only a little time and scarcely any money for the spreading of Christ's gospel.

How can anyone believe in the all-surpassing value of this gospel if you do not practice it, if you do not spread it, if you sacrifice neither your time nor your money for that purpose? . . .

But you, you are afraid of soiling your hands.

We certainly cannot afford to ignore such criticisms or shortcomings, but neither should we be daunted by them. After all, we have in our hands the divine solution if only we would use it, and it is this that I have continually tried to emphasize in developing all aspects of Christopher work.

I often think of the stark but still hopeful challenge that the poet W. H. Auden gave us at the beginning of World War II. Referring to "the waves of anger and fear" that "circulate over the bright and darkened lands of the earth, obsessing our private lives," he said: "We must love one another or die."

It is important therefore that all of us turn the spotlight on our own souls and humbly ask:

1. What can I do to share with others the divine love and truth that the Lord is sending to them through me?

2. How can I help those worse off spiritually, physically and economically than I am?

3. How can I do my part to bring about more efficient government, better quality education, higher principles in the home, business and labor, as well as raise the standards of literature, entertainment, and every other sphere of influence that shapes the destiny of mankind?

The message of Pope John XXIII to eighty thousand youths attending a convention in Stuttgart, Germany, in 1960, is a clear warning that we can and must answer those questions. The Holy Father cautioned the young people that their aim should be "not only to secure the eternal salvation of the human soul, but also to guarantee human dignity, liberty and peace here on earth."

Certainly the Lord has equipped each of us to play a decisive role in the temporal as well as spiritual welfare of mankind. Each of us is blessed with powers of mind, heart and soul that have scarcely been tapped. I was pointedly reminded of this while I sat next to a scientist at a dinner here in New York. In the course of conversation, I recounted some of the results that had come from the Christopher emphasis on the power and responsibility of each individual. The mere mention of every person's capacity for good brought about an immediate response from him. "You can't miss on this work that you're doing!" my dinner companion commented. "Our research has proved that the human mind is capable of storing up ten billion items of information. This means that, if a person absorbed twenty-five items every second during an eight-hour day, it would take forty years before his brain was filled. In the final analysis, facts themselves show that the stupidest person on the face of the earth is a potential genius."

Many years before, another scientist had carried this point one step further. Shortly before he died in 1923, the great electrical genius Charles P. Steinmetz said: "I think the greatest discovery will be along spiritual lines. Here is a force which history clearly teaches has been the greatest power in the development of man. Yet we have been merely playing with it and have never seriously studied it as we have the social forces. Some day people will learn that material things do not bring happiness, that they are of little use in making men creative and forceful."

It is thrilling to think that "the greatest discovery" of this or any age may yet come and that it will take place if and when enough individuals rediscover and put into practice the divine formula for world peace and justice given by God to

Moses thirty-two hundred years ago: "Love your neighbor as yourself." (Leviticus 19:18)

Although as old as revelation itself, this idea is still a "novel" one and relatively untried.

Part of the reason for this is that too many of us, as sons of Adam, settle for a selfish spiritual viewpoint that is more or less summed up by the man who said:

> God bless me and my wife,
> My son John and his wife,
> Us four,
> No more.

Until this attitude of "God and myself" shifts to "God, myself, and everyone else," we are not likely to get into the mainstream of life and champion both the human and divine rights of humanity.

The letter an eleven-year-old girl in San Francisco sent to me is a typical reminder that both young and old are somewhat aware that they should "get out of themselves" and *do* good rather than just *be* good.

She wrote: "Now please don't tell me to be a good little girl, say my prayers and obey my parents. I already do these things. I would like to do something more."

Short as it was, this child's note spoke volumes. I remember reading it when I spoke to the students at Foxcroft School in Middleburg, Virginia, at the invitation of its headmistress, Miss Charlotte Noland. The expressions on their faces assured me that the words had struck home. So I went on to remind them that there was "a bit of the missionary" in each of them and that, though they might not take it too seriously at the moment, they nevertheless had the power within them to do something worthwhile with their lives.

Then I told them about a doctor who claimed that most

people "amble through life" using only five per cent of their physical, mental and spiritual potential.

Finally I concluded: "I haven't the slightest idea what you girls *will* do with your lives, but it is thrilling to think of what you *could* do."

The greater the challenge and the larger the vision, the more likely people are to discover and put to use some of that 95 per cent potential that often goes untouched through an entire lifetime.

I often think of the striking instance of this that was told in a Christopher Award-winning book entitled *Endurance*, the story of the Antarctic expedition led by Sir Ernest Shackleton in 1914. At one point in the telling, the author, Alfred Lansing, quotes the following brief advertisement that was placed in a London newspaper prior to the trip:

> Men wanted for hazardous journey—small wages,
> bitter cold, long months of complete darkness,
> constant danger, safe return doubtful. Honor
> and recognition in case of success.

Despite the frank reference to difficulties, that four-line want ad brought five thousand answers. Only twenty-eight men were finally chosen, but judging from the response, there must have been tens of thousands of others who were caught, at least momentarily, by the idea that they could play a big part in an important undertaking.

Greatness of outlook and purpose can inspire anyone to reach beyond the narrow confines of a kitchen, classroom, factory or office to contribute to the common good of all. But more and more individuals are beginning to realize that without the major ingredient of divine motivation they will never experience true fulfillment or satisfaction.

This point certainly stands out in the following anonymous

letter I received from a person who had apparently received the *Christopher News Notes* from a friend:

I am an agnostic—and my first thought upon receiving your *News Notes* was to tear them up without reading them.

However, because I love to read and perhaps partly out of curiosity, I have been reading them through. Although I may never be able to really believe in a God—I feel that I have learned a great deal from what you have written. I do try to live a good life—be thoughtful, considerate, etc.—in other words—live the Golden Rule. But your words make me want to do more—really devote more time to helping others less fortunate than I. I wish I could believe, for I hate myself and the life I've created for my children, and how I wish I had a faith—for comfort, perhaps, and hopefully, even, for guidance.

Enough of that. Thank you for sending me your *News Notes* and even if they convert no one, be assured that they have helped in great measure at least one person.

The letter was signed simply: "A friend."

All too many people are hampered by this lack of fulfillment in their lives. One young man described it this way: "I have no set goal, and not having any big purpose in my life is an awful feeling. It is a wandering emptiness."

To help individuals like this find and apply the missing ingredient they are looking for should be a privilege and incentive for anyone. It certainly has been all of that and much more for me.

As the Christopher idea develops, it becomes more fascinating, more challenging, and more consoling:

—fascinating because it demonstrates what individuals will do when they realize, often for the first time, how needed they are in God's plan and how important it is for them to fulfill that mission that has been assigned to no one else;

—challenging because of the seemingly inexhaustible possibilities that are presented as this realization spreads to more and more individuals;

—consoling because, as one person after another is imbued with this sense of mission, they help strengthen and deepen the roots on which the full flowering of Christianity inevitably depends.

The one reminder that seems to be most effective in stimulating this sense of mission is that what we accomplish here on earth will count for all eternity. In every talk, broadcast and piece of writing, I try to make at least one reference to the fact that we will have to render an account of our stewardship before the Judgment Seat.

The widespread desire to do something in preparation for eternity is plainly evident in the big volume of post cards and letters that come to Christopher headquarters. One of the most impressive reactions followed a full-page feature by *This Week* magazine that highlighted eight excerpts from the 1963 Christopher calendar. Immediately afterwards, we received more than seven thousand requests for copies of the calendar. The saying most often referred to by those writing us was this one by Stephen Grellet: "I shall pass this way but once; any good that I can do, or any kindness that I can show, let me do it now. Let me not defer or neglect it, for I shall not pass this way again."

Anyone like myself who gets involved in missionary work is soon caught up by its divine magnetism. In becoming more and more aware that he is a tiny instrument, however unworthy, through which God's power can reach others, he naturally experiences a degree of fulfillment and satisfaction. But it is not a satisfaction that comes from his own efforts. It is one that comes from realizing he has been a "connecting link" in helping others to play their own individual roles as God's agents in changing the world for the better.

To see what individuals accomplish when their thoughts, prayers, words and actions are motivated by a Christlike purpose reacts on me like a divine stimulant. It becomes almost effortless to try to do more and more which could encourage others to be Christbearers.

Not everyone understands the continual fascination of the many-faceted ramifications of this dynamic idea, as was quite evident from the remark one friend of mine made. I had been spending a short time at his home while working on a new Christopher pamphlet. Late one afternoon, he asked if I would stop pounding the typewriter for a while and take a walk with him. He had been working, too, and wanted a little change of pace.

As we started out, I began telling him about some Christopher projects on the planning board, thinking that he would have some good suggestions for developing them. He listened for a few minutes as we went down the road. Finally, he turned and said: "Look, can't you forget work for a while—all you do is eat, drink and sleep the Christophers!"

He was right, I had to admit, but as far as I am concerned, being "wrapped up" in Christopher work is easy to explain. The more it expands the more evident it becomes that we have scarcely scratched the surface. The possibilities awaiting future development hold tremendous and exciting promise. While rejoicing in what has been done, it is certainly no time to relax.

In the next few decades, issues that involve the temporal and eternal destiny of most of mankind will be at stake. We cannot ignore the towering problems to be faced.

A hundred million and more in our very midst are not being effectively reached by any religion, and yet are being bombarded on all sides by the deceptive allurements of deadly materialism. Two billion persons over the world have yet to hear of the true God. Three quarters of humanity live in dehumanizing poverty. A quarter of a billion of the children of the earth receive no formal schooling. Until each of us recognizes that these problems are "my business as much as anyone's," little progress will be made.

Communism still forges ahead because its adherents, whether in low position or high, are convinced that they personally can play a vital role in reshaping the future of the world.

Nikita Khrushchev underlined this bigness of vision and driving sense of urgency when he said in Villach, Austria, June 5, 1960: "Life is short and I want to see the Red flag fly over the whole world in my lifetime."

The fact that he used the words "whole world" caught my attention. Nearly two thousand years have passed since Christ told His followers: "Go into the whole world and preach the gospel to every creature." (Mark 16:15)

Dare we, as His followers, any longer ignore His command and challenge to bring His love and truth to all humanity?

The simple idea behind the Christopher movement is based on that command and challenge—that everyone, without exception, should be "a man with a mission" and do his part to integrate the principles of the gospel into the whole of life.

It was this idea that was in the back of my mind when I joined Maryknoll forty-two years ago, though at that time I expected it would take me to the fields afar.

I never dreamed that I would be spending most of my priestly life trying to reach anyone and everyone with its dynamic possibilities from an office in the heart of Manhattan. Nor did I have even the vaguest notion that my own life would be so fully enriched in the process.

I often think of the truth of the Master's divine paradox: "Everyone who has left house, or brothers, or sisters, or father, or mother, or wife, or children, or lands, for my name's sake, shall receive a hundredfold and shall possess life ever-lasting." (Matthew 19:29)

As I look back, it seems to me that I have received far more than the promised "hundredfold." The fun and consolations have far outweighed the relatively small efforts I have made as the Lord's "errand boy."

Instances such as the ones cited in these few chapters have been a continuing and exciting experience. It has been a source of never ending joy to play even a minor part in help-ing others to discover that they, too, are called to be God's collaborators in applying His love and truth to the running of human affairs.

What has been accomplished thus far by this "everyone can be a missioner" idea is only the beginning. It is just a slight preview of the hopeful transformation that can take place both here and throughout the world once enough people are captivated by the conviction that they can "light a candle" instead of "curse the darkness."

Many years ago in St. Paul, Minnesota, I tried to sum up the timelessness and universality of this apostolic concept. I had been telling an audience some of the ways that individuals in all sorts of circumstances had been putting the missionary idea to work. During the question period that followed, one elderly lady who was obviously impressed by the hopeful ex-amples exclaimed:

"What a wonderful idea this is! When did it start and where did it come from?"

I paused for a moment and then explained that Our Lord and Saviour, Jesus Christ, had given mankind the divine for-mula nearly two thousand years ago. All the Christopher movement is trying to do is to encourage people to apply it to modern times. The idea is far from new or original—it is as old as the hills of Galilee.